# STAR
# THE
# CLONE
# WARS
# WARS

## THE OFFICIAL EPISODE GUIDE · SEASON 1

**Written by Jason Fry**
**Compiled and edited by Rob Valois**

Based on the TV series *STAR WARS: THE CLONE WARS*

Grosset & Dunlap · LucasBooks

GROSSET & DUNLAP
Published by the Penguin Group
Penguin Group (USA) Inc., 375 Hudson Street, New York, New York 10014, USA
Penguin Group (Canada), 90 Eglinton Avenue East, Suite 700,
Toronto, Ontario M4P 2Y3, Canada (a division of Pearson Penguin Canada Inc.)
Penguin Books Ltd., 80 Strand, London WC2R 0RL, England
Penguin Group Ireland, 25 St. Stephen's Green, Dublin 2, Ireland
(a division of Penguin Books Ltd.)
Penguin Group (Australia), 250 Camberwell Road,
Camberwell, Victoria 3124, Australia (a division of Pearson Australia Group Pty. Ltd.)
Penguin Books India Pvt. Ltd., 11 Community Centre, Panchsheel Park,
New Delhi—110 017, India
Penguin Group (NZ), 67 Apollo Drive, Rosedale, North Shore 0632, New Zealand
(a division of Pearson New Zealand Ltd.)
Penguin Books (South Africa) (Pty.) Ltd., 24 Sturdee Avenue,
Rosebank, Johannesburg 2196, South Africa

Penguin Books Ltd., Registered Offices:
80 Strand, London WC2R 0RL, England

This book is published in partnership with LucasBooks, a division of Lucasfilm Ltd.

ISBN 978-0-448-45247-0          10 9 8 7 6 5 4 3 2 1

# STAR WARS
# THE CLONE WARS
# WARS

## THE OFFICIAL EPISODE GUIDE • SEASON 1

# TABLE OF CONTENTS

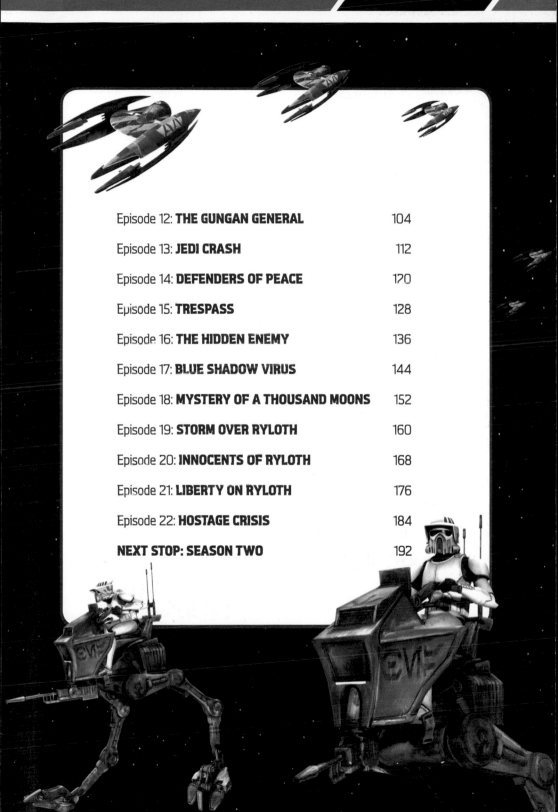

## The Movie:

A PADAWAN WOULD JUST SLOW ME DOWN.

# STAR WARS: THE CLONE WARS

A long time ago in a galaxy far, far away....

**Original Release Date:**
8/15/08

**Written by** Henry Gilroy,
Steven Melching, Scott Murphy

**Directed by** Dave Filoni

**Cast**
Matt Lanter:
    Anakin Skywalker
James Arnold Taylor:
    Obi-Wan Kenobi, 4A-7
Ashley Eckstein:
    Ahsoka Tano
Tom Kane:
    Yoda, Admiral Wulff
    Yularen, narrator
Christopher Lee:
    Count Dooku
Dee Bradley Baker:
    Clone troopers
Samuel L. Jackson:
    Mace Windu
Nika Futterman:
    TC-70, Asajj Ventress
Anthony Daniels:
    C-3PO

# SYNOPSIS

During the battle for Christophsis, Anakin and Obi-Wan are surprised when Anakin's new Padawan, Ahsoka, arrives. Together, Anakin and his new apprentice destroy a Separatist shield generator while Obi-Wan stalls the attacks by negotiating a fake surrender to General Whorm Loathsom.

After the Separatist defeat, Yoda sends Obi-Wan to meet with Jabba the Hutt, whose son, Rotta, has been kidnapped. Meanwhile, Anakin and Ahsoka head to the planet Teth to look for the missing Huttlet. However, it's a trap. Dooku arranged the kidnapping and plans to blame it on the Jedi. Asajj Ventress tries to stop the Jedi, but she fails and allows Ahsoka and Anakin to escape.

On Coruscant, Padmé pays a visit to Jabba's uncle, Ziro. She learns that he conspired with Dooku to kidnap the baby.

On Tatooine, Anakin and Ahsoka defeat Dooku and his MagnaGuards and bring Rotta to Jabba. The Hutt threatens to kill the Jedi, but frees them when he learns that his uncle was responsible for the kidnapping.

# NEWSREEL

A galaxy divided! Striking swiftly after the Battle of Geonosis, Count Dooku's droid army has seized control of the major hyperspace lanes, separating the Republic from the majority of its clone army. With few clones available, the Jedi generals cannot gain a foothold on the Outer Rim as more and more planets choose to join Dooku's Separatists. While the Jedi are occupied fighting a war, no one is left to keep the peace. Chaos and crime spread, and the innocent become victims in a lawless galaxy. Crime lord Jabba the Hutt's son has been kidnapped by a rival band of pirates. Desperate to save his son, Jabba puts out a call for help—a call the Jedi are cautious to answer.... ▮

## ANAKIN'S PADAWAN

A lot of fans were surprised to learn that Anakin Skywalker would have an apprentice during the Clone Wars. As it turned out, Ahsoka Tano would let the storytellers explore the differences between her and Anakin and examine Anakin's emotional attachments and how they will shape his destiny.

**Cast (Continued)**
Ian Abercrombie:
    Chancellor Palpatine, Darth Sidious
Catherine Taber:
    Padmé Amidala
Corey Burton:
    Whorm Loathsom, Ziro the Hutt, KRONOS-327
David Acord:
    Rotta
Kevin Michael Richardson:
    Jabba the Hutt
Matthew Wood:
    Battle droids

**Locations:** Christophsis, Coruscant, Teth, Tatooine

**Vehicles:** *Resolute* (*Venator*-class Star Destroyer), *Acclamator I*-class assault ship, All Terrain Tactical Enforcer (AT-TE), Armored Assault Tank (AAT), Delta-7B *Aethersprite*-class starfighter, *Twilight* (G9 Rigger), Republic attack gunship, *Munificent*-class star frigate, *Nu*-class attack shuttle, *Punworcca*-class interstellar sloop, V-19 Torrent starfighter

**Weapons:** DC-15A blaster, DC-15S blaster, DC-17 hand blaster, E-5 blaster rifle, electrostaff

## Obi-Wan Kenobi

Equally respected for his skill in battles and negotiations, Obi-Wan Kenobi was Anakin Skywalker's master until his Padawan passed the trials and became a Jedi Knight.

## CHARACTERS

> YOU'RE RECKLESS, LITTLE ONE. YOU NEVER WOULD HAVE MADE IT AS OBI-WAN'S PADAWAN . . . BUT YOU MIGHT MAKE IT AS MINE.

## ANAKIN'S PADAWAN (cont'd)

Series writer Henry Gilroy says that before their first story meeting with George Lucas, he and supervising director Dave Filoni had discussed bringing in a female Jedi. With Anakin promoted to Jedi Knight, they thought, Obi-Wan Kenobi might train a new Padawan.

"George was way ahead of us and explained how he wanted Anakin to have a Padawan," he says. "Dave and I were shocked initially, but then after our discussions with George, we realized how many great storytelling opportunities Anakin's Padawan would provide. For example, Anakin would have to mature and develop more patience and responsibility if he's going to set a proper example for her. Dave and I originally wrote Ahsoka

## WEAPON PROFILE

### Lightsaber

The weapon of a Jedi Knight, its hilt emits a blade of pure energy focused by a crystal.

as more tentative and naïve—growing up in the Temple, she would be a little more uncertain and insecure as she's suddenly exposed to the great big galaxy—but George wanted to expand her character into a feisty spitfire who could give Princess Leia a run for her money."

Gilroy says he and Filoni proposed the character as a Togruta and named her Ashla, after a Togruta youngling spied in *Attack of the Clones*. But Ashla's bid for immortality fizzled almost as soon as Lucas heard the name, Gilroy recalls: "Right there at the table, he pulled a history book off his bookshelf and he thumbed through it. He changed her name to Ahsoka, after Ashoka, an emperor of ancient India."

## CAPTAIN REX

Dave Filoni says the steady Captain Rex was originally going to be Alpha, an ARC trooper introduced by Dark Horse Comics, who showed his mettle during battles on Kamino and in the

## PLANET PROFILE
### Christophsis

**Region:** Outer Rim

**Inhabitants:** Humans, servant species

Christophsis is a world of crystal spires. Its people became immensely rich by mining asteroids in the system's outer reaches.

## ALIEN PROFILE
### Togrutas

Togrutas evolved from predators, and their colorful skins were originally used to confuse prey. They have two hollow montrals growing from the top of the skull and "head tails" that fall over the chest and back. Togrutas preserve some of their native traditions as Jedi, wearing elaborate costumes and trophies.

## CAPTAIN REX (cont'd)

Naboo system. But George Lucas noted that Anakin, Ahsoka, R2 (Artoo), and Alpha would make for a lot of As, and *Star Wars*'s version of *The A-Team* was no more. (Lucas provided the new name.) As for the scar below Rex's lower lip, it's a tip of the fedora to a similar scar on Harrison Ford's chin, a mark made part of the *Indiana Jones* saga.

Rex also has a bit of Jango Fett in him—witness the scene on Christophsis where he blazes away with two pistols at once. "We wanted the clones to have certain tendencies that Jango did, and this type of pistol-wielding is something that we saw Jango doing," Filoni says. "So Rex is definitely one of the clones who's a little more Jango than some of the other guys. When a clone gets to a point where they're almost a little bit renegade, they refer to it

### Captain Rex

A veteran of many battles, the elite clone Rex is Anakin Skywalker's gruff, no-nonsense second-in-command, and is as brave and headstrong as the Jedi he serves.

as 'gone Jango.' So that's kind of a fun thing to have."

As a character, Rex calms Anakin down—he's a link between the Jedi Knight's superhuman abilities and the clones' simple bravery. And like the audience, he at first doubts and then accepts Ahsoka. It's Rex who lectures Ahsoka that experience is what counts in the Republic Army, but it's also Rex who tells her she did a good job after the droid army's shield generator is destroyed.

Rex also let Filoni explore an idea that had interested him for a while: that the Jedi would have an effect on the clones, encouraging their individuality and at the same time shaping their personalities.

"Rex is obviously a little bit more like Anakin," he says, adding that the clones take on some of the traits of the Jedi who train them. "So Rex is a little more gruff, and a little more intense."

## SOMETHING BORROWED

Many ideas in the *Star Wars* saga have had to wait for their moment. The name Mace Windu dates back to drafts from 1973, Cloud City was first imagined as a city on Alderaan, and *Revenge of the Sith*'s juggernaut dates back to concept sketches for *The Empire Strikes Back*. *The Clone Wars* movie continues this

## ALIEN PROFILE
### Hutts

Hutts are mighty amphibians that have controlled a large part of the galaxy for thousands of years, making handsome profits from shady businesses such as spice smuggling and slavery. Hutts are ruthless and greedy, and see themselves as the only species worthy of respect in the galaxy. Their clans compete ferociously over markets and the smallest points of honor.

## PLANET PROFILE
### Teth

**Region:** Wild Space

Teth was first settled as a Hutt vacation spot, but abandoned after it became the scene of too many clan vendettas. It is dotted with abandoned monasteries and Hutt palaces.

## VEHICLE PROFILE
### AT-TE

**Model:** All-Terrain Tactical Enforcer

**Class:** Walker

**Weapons:**
• Laser cannons
• Concussion warheads

## DROID PROFILE
### Retail Droid

Properly known as LR-57 combat droids, these hulking droids like to bury themselves, wait for an enemy to walk overhead, and then explode out of the ground in ambush.

## SOMETHING BORROWED (cont'd)

tradition, giving new life to concepts that didn't quite fit into earlier movies. Dave Filoni notes that the look of the Kerkoiden general Whorm Loathsom is inspired by Doug Chiang's art for *The Phantom Menace*'s Neimoidians. That entrance to the monastery on Teth? It's an adaptation of a Ralph McQuarrie design for Jabba's palace. The headgear worn by Padmé during her ill-fated visit to Ziro the Hutt's Coruscant club was originally supposed to appear in *Attack of the Clones*. Those drum-headed retail droids Ahsoka

### Jabba the Hutt

A crime lord of the Desilijic family, Jabba controls a number of Outer Rim trade routes. His support could help tip the Clone Wars to the Republic or the Separatists.

runs into on Christophsis? They were an early version of Episode I's destroyer droids, also by Chiang. And then there's the *Twilight*, wryly referred to by Filoni as "the Winnebago of *Star Wars*." Before making its debut in *The Clone Wars*, the freighter was an Erik Tiemens design for a firefighting ship in *Revenge of the Sith*.

"George often gives us old, abandoned designs, and then we adapt them into new races of aliens or new robots," Filoni says. "And that's kind of fun to do."

## A VERTICAL BATTLE

When it comes to intergalactic duking it out, the *Star Wars* saga has seen it all: thrilling dogfights above space stations, chases through asteroid belts, trench warfare on an ice world, ship-to-ship combat in the upper reaches of a

# Rotta

Rotta is Jabba's young son, and as cranky and smelly as one would expect a Huttlet to be. Jabba calls him his "pedunkee mufkin," and treats his son with rare tenderness.

YOU'LL HAVE TO DO BETTER THAN THAT, MY DARLING.

## ALIEN PROFILE

### Kerkoidens

Kerkoidens are known as clever traders and canny politicians. Many feel a bit embarrassed about their long claws and sharp teeth, and often take pains to appear as refined and sophisticated as possible.

## VEHICLE PROFILE

### Republic Attack Gunship

**Model:** Rothana Heavy Engineering

**Class:** Repulsor lift gunship

**Weapons:**
- Laser turrets
- Air-to-air rockets
- Missle launchers

## A VERTICAL BATTLE (cont'd)

planet's atmosphere, and scorched-earth battles on grassy plains and in red-hued badlands. But until *The Clone Wars*, Jedi Knights had never had to defy gravity, fighting their way up a cliff as battle droids pour laser fire down on their heads.

The "up-the-cliff" battle on Teth began with a location—George Lucas introduced a new dimension when he told *The Clone Wars* team that he wanted the abandoned monastery on top of a mesa in a jungle. (Teth was originally a rock planet—as Dave Filoni notes, "Rocks were a lot easier for us to do at the time.")

"When he put the palace on top of the mesa, Henry Gilroy said, 'Well, there goes your tank battle,'" Filoni recalls. "But I thought, 'Well, let's just put the tank battle on the side of the cliff.' It really addressed a couple of problems. When you do something in *Star Wars*, you have to present it in a new way to the audience, and this was a way to make it more dynamic and more exciting than we had seen."

The switch, Filoni says, "changed the whole dynamic of the battle," from the shots of the droids looking down the cliff at the advancing clones to the surprise of seeing the Republic's walkers do more than you thought they could.

# GALACTIC DISPATCHES
## CHRISTOPHSIS

One of the Outer Rim's richest planets, Christophsis is a world of huge crystal spires, around which the Christophsians (originally humans from the Core Worlds) have built their cold and beautiful cities.

The Christophsians became rich when they figured out how to mine the whirling asteroids of their system, which are filled with rare metals. They stayed rich by manipulating the galaxy's markets and protecting their technological secrets, as well as hiring the most expensive Vippit lawyers to sue anyone who tried to copy their techniques or strike deals with their trading partners. Few visitors to Christophsis were allowed to land on the planet itself—even high-ranking members of the Mining Guild met the Christophsians on space stations in the asteroid belts. Those who did see Christophsis said the Christophsians lived lives of luxury, with poor humans serving as household servants.

Life on Christophsis was disrupted by a Separatist invasion and a Republic counter-attack that left several Christophsian cities in splinters. Most in the Republic cheered the defeat of a Separatist advance that could have left the Jedi and clone troopers cut off from the Core. But many also hid a smile at the sight of clone boots tramping over Christophsian ruins. Honestly, it couldn't have happened to a nicer planet.

# Episode 1:

# AMBUSH

"Great leaders inspire greatness in others."

SMALLER IN NUMBER WE ARE, BUT LARGER IN MIND . . .

## SYNOPSIS

Jedi Master Yoda and a team of clone troopers have been sent to the system of Toydaria to convince the Toydarian King Katuunko to join the Galactic Republic. However, Count Dooku has sent the assassin Asajj Ventress to negotiate the Separatist's own deal with Katuunko. Above the moon of Rugosa, Yoda is ambushed by Separatist forces, sending the Jedi Master and his clone escorts into a race against time to defeat Ventress's droid army and prove the Republic's worth to King Katuunko.

**Original Airdate:** 10/3/08

**Written by** Stephen Melching

**Directed by** Dave Bullock

**Cast**
Tom Kane:
    Yoda, narrator
Dee Bradley Baker:
    Clone troopers
Brian George:
    King Katuunko
Corey Burton:
    Count Dooku
Nika Futterman:
    Asajj Ventress
Matthew Wood:
    Battle droids

**Location:** Rugosa

**Vehicles:** Republic frigate, *Munificent*-class star frigate, C-9979 landing craft, Armored Assault Tank (AAT), Republic gunship, Toydarian star yacht, *Punworcca*-class interstellar sloop

## NEWSREEL

A galaxy divided by war! Peaceful worlds must choose sides or face the threat of invasion. Republic and Separatist armies vie for the allegiance of neutral planets. Desperate to build a Republic supply base on the system of Toydaria, Jedi Master Yoda travels to secret negotiations on a remote neutral moon.... ∎

## THE LOOK OF RUGOSA

Supervising director Dave Filoni says that for the early episodes of *The Clone Wars*, he wanted to have "a different look for every planet." To continue the tradition of the *Star Wars* franchise, each planet would have a single kind of terrain, instead of being a patchwork like the Earth. (Think of the *Star Wars* saga's desert planets, ice worlds, forest moons, and lava worlds, for instance.) The design team was inspired by old film serials such as *Flash Gordon*. For "Ambush," Filoni says he wanted a

**Weapons:** Lightsaber, DC-15A blaster rifle, DC-15S blaster, grenade, E-5 blaster rifle, Z-6 rotary blaster cannon, rocket launcher, Toydarian ceremonial sword, electrobinoculars

## CHARACTERS

Count Dooku
Trooper Jek
King Katuunko
Trooper Rys
Lieutenant Thire
Asajj Ventress
Yoda

## EPISODE HIGHLIGHT

## Asajj Ventress

Count Dooku's most trusted assassin. Though she's not officially a Sith apprentice, Ventress has clearly been well-trained in the arts of lightsaber dueling and Force manipulation.

## EPISODE HIGHLIGHT

OKAY, CLANKERS. SUCK LASER!

YOUR HELMETS, REMOVE THEM. YOUR FACES, I WISH TO SEE.

THERE'S NOT MUCH TO LOOK AT HERE, SIR. WE ALL SHARE THE SAME FACE.

DECEIVE YOU, EYES CAN. IN THE FORCE, VERY DIFFERENT EACH ONE OF YOU ARE.

## THE LOOK OF RUGOSA (cont'd)

"new way to look at a planet in *Star Wars*," so he made "a short list of what hasn't been done by George already—as he'll tell you, he's done them all. Or at least the easy ones, he'll tell me."

Looking at the list gave him the idea of making Rugosa a "coral moon," with seas that had dried out long ago. Filoni made several concept paintings of scenes on Rugosa to explore what he wanted, and says concept artist Russell Chong did "a great job" creating a wealth of different-looking corals—which added to the faintly sad, eerily beautiful look of Rugosa.

"I especially wanted shots where there'd be little rays of light coming down through the coral bed and giving a dappled look to the ground," Filoni says.

By the way, Rugosa was originally red, but that idea was discarded because a red sun would light much of the action in "Rising *Malevolence*."

"I also like to create different color themes," Filoni says.

## TRIVIA

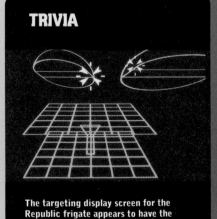

The targeting display screen for the Republic frigate appears to have the same orange-against-red grid seen aboard the *Millennium Falcon* in *A New Hope*.

## NOT ALL THE SAME

A sad note in "Ambush" comes when Yoda asks his clones to take off their helmets so he can see their faces, causing them to hesitate and Lieutenant Thire to remark: "Not much to look at here, sir. We all share the same face."

But not to Yoda. "Deceive you, eyes can," he says gently. "In the Force, very different each one of you are."

That theme runs through the series: Are the clones living droids, or individual humans? Yoda insists they're individuals, even though the clones themselves seem to doubt that's true.

"Very early on, George wanted to explore the clones as individuals, suggesting

## VEHICLE PROFILE
### Republic Frigate

**Model:** Refitted *Consular*-class cruiser

**Class:** Frigate

**Weapons:**
- Twin light turbolaser cannon batteries
- Point-defense medium laser cannons

## Rys, Thire, and Jek

Members of the Coruscant Guard whose duty it is to protect Yoda on his diplomatic mission to Rugosa.

I ASK, HOW CAN A JEDI PROTECT YOU IF THEY CANNOT PROTECT THEMSELVES?

## ALIEN PROFILE
## Toydarians

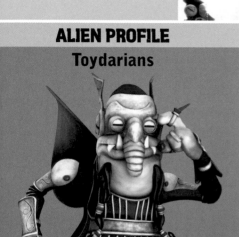

Toydarians are winged species from the planet Toydaria. They are typically short with small trunks and tusks on their faces and birdlike legs that end in webbed feet. They can fly quite quickly, and prefer flight to walking.

## TRIVIA

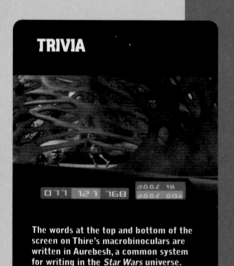

The words at the top and bottom of the screen on Thire's macrobinoculars are written in Aurebesh, a common system for writing in the *Star Wars* universe. They read: "Infrared Mode" on the top and "Regular Mode" on the bottom.

### NOT ALL THE SAME (cont'd)

personalized haircuts, tattoos, and armor paint jobs," Henry Gilroy says, adding that "we often gave them names that reflected their character— In 'Rising *Malevolence*,' 'Sinker' was the pessimist and 'Boost' was the optimistic one. The clones were well trained in the art of war, but lacked experience in social interaction. The idea that the Jedi imprinted on them and were able to expand the clones' view of their purpose and why they were fighting was very interesting. In a sense, the Jedi were fathers, by example teaching the clones honorable and compassionate behavior, which we will start to see many clones demonstrate on their own as the war goes on."

"In 'Ambush,'" Gilroy says, "one clone was preoccupied with weapons, another with how many of the enemy they would face, and the commander was single-minded about completing the mission at any cost. Yoda took the time to help them realize they were seeing a narrow aspect of the war and he opened their eyes to the bigger philosophical picture. We wanted to bring back our favorite version of Yoda, the wise old sage who was full of wisdom, yet could more than carry his own in battle."

## WATTO AND KATUUNKO

In "Ambush," viewers meet Katuunko, the Toydarian king—who's quite different from Watto, the Mos Espa junk dealer who owns Anakin and Shmi Skywalker in Episode I: *The Phantom Menace.* (And who seems to have fallen on hard times by Episode II: *Attack of the Clones.*)

Dave Filoni says the character of Watto was helpful in imagining what Katuunko and other Toydarians would be like—but these new Toydarians wouldn't resemble him too closely.

"He's a character," Filoni says of Watto. "He's on Tatooine. What are the Toydarians like who are actually on Toydaria? You have to quickly identify that Watto's actually the odd guy out—he's the guy selling parts in the shop. That's his life." For whatever reason, Filoni says, Watto "has fallen way far out of that culture."

**WEAPON PROFILE**

## Z-6 Rotary Blaster Cannon

A powerful, rotating blaster

# King Katuunko

The ruler of the system of Toydaria and its moon Rugosa. The winged Toydarians' minds are able to resist all types of Jedi mind tricks.

## DROID PROFILE

### Destroyer Droid

Also known as droidekas, these killer droids curl up and roll like wheels until they reach their targets, when they uncurl, raise shields, and open fire.

## WATTO AND KATUUNKO (cont'd)

This isn't just a lesson for Toydarian characters. With any *Star Wars* species, Filoni says, "you have to give variety. You can't prescribe the same traits to all the characters. So with the king, we thought, 'Well, Watto was growing a beard—let's give him a beard. Watto had a broken tooth, but this guy's not going to have that.'"

Katuunko's beard was much neater, and tied into little braids; his teeth weren't broken; and he had what Filoni calls "a little Wagnerian-style helmet with little wings."

## Yoda

At nearly nine hundred years old, Yoda is without peer in his knowledge of the Force. He wields his lightsaber with blinding speed and uses his agility to render himself nearly invulnerable.

# GALACTIC DISPATCHES
## THE FATE OF RUGOSA

The Toydarians are native to Hutt Space, and have served the Hutts for thousands of years. But they like to keep secrets from their masters. Centuries before *The Clone Wars*, Toydarian scouts exploring space near the Balmorra Run discovered Rugosa, an uninhabited moon with warm swamps and shallow, coral-filled seas. To the Toydarians, that felt like paradise, and the planet's clan chiefs turned Rugosa into a vacation spot.

The Hutts were angry when they discovered the sun they called Gash Rugosa and the planet orbiting it, and decided to punish the Toydarians. The Hutts released an ancient plague on Rugosa, one that dried up its seas within months. The Toydarians' playground was ruined, transformed into a dry world where coral fans dotted the floor of the vanished ocean.

Yoda had been saddened to hear what the cruel Hutts had done to the coral moon. But he quickly saw reasons to hope. Many plants and tough corals had survived, and rainfall was slowing filling up the deepest parts of Rugosa's seas again. And fluttering through the coral forests were baby neebray manta—the great gas gulpers had made the moon part of their migration route through space. Despite all the Hutts had done to it, life was returning to Rugosa.

# Episode 2:

KOH-TO-YA, LITTLE 'SOKA.

# RISING MALEVOLENCE

"Belief is not a matter of choice, but of conviction."

**Original Airdate:** 10/3/08

**Written by** Stephen Melching

**Directed by** Dave Filoni

**Cast**
Matt Lanter:
    Anakin Skywalker
Ashley Eckstein:
    Ahsoka Tano
James Arnold Taylor:
    Obi-Wan Kenobi, Plo Koon
Dee Bradley Baker:
    Clone troopers
Tom Kane:
    Yoda, Admiral Yularen,
    narrator
Corey Burton:
    Count Dooku
Terrence "TC" Carson:
    Mace Windu
Ian Abercrombie:
    Chancellor Palpatine
Tim Brock:
    Medical droid
Matthew Wood:
    General Grievous, battle
    droids

## SYNOPSIS

In the Abregado system, Jedi Master Plo Koon's cruiser is attacked by General Grievous and the Separatists' secret new warship, the *Malevolence*. Anakin and Ahsoka set out, against the Council's wishes, to rescue Plo. Meanwhile, Plo and his clones are fighting for their lives in an escape pod as droid pod hunters slice their way through the debris. Arriving in the nick of time, Anakin and Ahsoka make the rescue and escape before the *Malevolence* can stop them—leaving Grievous to answer to Count Dooku.

# NEWSREEL

The clone starfleet is under siege! Dozens of Republic warships have been destroyed in merciless surprise attacks that leave no survivors. Rumors spread of a terrible new Separatist weapon. In the face of growing fear, the Jedi Council sends Master Plo Koon to hunt down the menace before it strikes again.... ∎

**Locations:** Abregado, Coruscant

**Vehicles:** *Twilight* (G9 Rigger), V-19 Torrent starfighter, *Triumphant* (*Venator*-class Star Destroyer), Separatist boarding craft, V-19 torrent starfighter, *Malevolence* (*Subjugator*-class heavy cruiser), Republic attack gunship, pod hunter

**Weapons:** DC-15S blaster, E-5 blaster rifle, ion cannon, lightsaber

## A DIRECTOR'S FAVORITE

Dave Filoni is a big fan of the Kel Dor Jedi Master Plo Koon, and worked on many aspects of the character for his reintroduction in *The Clone Wars*, from his language to his ability to survive—briefly—in outer space.

Take "koh-to-ya," the Kel Dorian phrase with which Plo Koon greets Ahsoka—and which she answers back. That bit of alien language does more than give the viewer a feel for Kel Dorian—it also shows there's a bond between Ahsoka and Plo Koon.

## CHARACTERS

Trooper Boost
Count Dooku
General Grievous
Obi-Wan Kenobi
Plo Koon
Chancellor Palpatine
R2-D2
Sergeant Sinker
Anakin Skywalker
Ahsoka Tano
TB-2
Mace Windu
Commander Wolffe
Yoda
Admiral Wullf Yularen

# Ahsoka Tano

Anakin Skywalker's young Padawan, Ahsoka Tano is headstrong and independent . . . much like her Master.

## EPISODE HIGHLIGHT

BOLDLY SPOKEN FOR ONE SO YOUNG.

SHE IS LEARNING FROM ANAKIN.

## VEHICLE PROFILE

### Malevolence

**Model:** *Subjugator*-class heavy cruiser

**Class:** Heavy cruiser

**Weapons:**
- T2 ion pulse cannons
- Twin turbolaser batteries

## A DIRECTOR'S FAVORITE (cont'd)

"That was something that allowed you, early in the episode, to go, 'Wait a minute, Ahsoka knows how to speak to Plo Koon in this weird language, what's that about?'"

Filoni says, "It hints at the idea that she knows Plo Koon, actually better than Anakin does."

As Filoni explains, "It's also a leftover from when I experimented with Plo Koon just speaking Kel Dorian and what that was going to sound like. We had a couple of different ideas for how we could create this language. My wife is heavy into language, and she'd been studying Gaelic. And so we thought we'd take some Gaelic language and write it backward and read it—maybe that would work."

The problem, though, is that a weird-sounding language makes it harder for the audience to develop real feelings for a character. Filoni says that "there are a lot of exceptions—Artoo, Chewbacca, they're able to have a lot of emotions—but Plo Koon had to have a lot of important dialogue when he spoke with his clones. So, in the end, I changed it to English. And that launched this other whole debate: How is he going to sound when he speaks English?"

Filoni and Henry Gilroy had originally imagined Plo Koon as a very strict Jedi, and imagined patterning him after the samurai seen in the films of Akira Kurosawa, which were a strong influence on George Lucas. But Filoni decided on a new direction instead: "I wanted him to feel ancient and wise, like you can't tell how old he is. I felt a lot of the Council probably was like that, and it gives him a lot of depth, a lot of history."

The voice, Filoni says, took more than a month to get right. "The first thing you encounter is that any really deep voice that's highly modified ends up sounding like Darth Vader," he says. "And George really wants Vader to stand alone as far as that iconic voice."

## WEAPON PROFILE
### Ion Cannon

Fires highly ionized particles that interfere with the operation of electronics and computer systems

## VEHICLE PROFILE
### *Jedi Cruiser*

**Model:** *Venator*-class Star Destroyer

**Class:** Capital Ship

**Weapons:**
- Heavy turbolasers
- Torpedoes
- Fighter complement

## Plo Koon
Kel Dor Jedi Master from the planet of Dorin, Plo Koon is a skilled warrior and member of the Jedi High Council.

## VEHICLE PROFILE
### Twilight

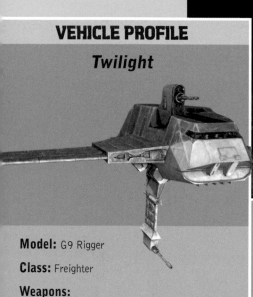

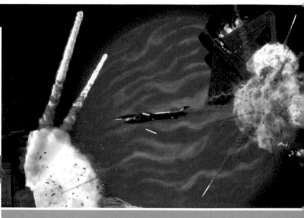

**Model:** G9 Rigger

**Class:** Freighter

**Weapons:**
- Three heavy blasters
- Rotating laser cannon with periscope control

## ALIEN PROFILE
### Kel Dors

Sometimes referred to as Kel Dorians, this species comes from the planet Dorin in the Expansion Region. Because of the low oxygen atmosphere of their homeworld, Kel Dors must wear protective masks and goggles to shield them in oxygen-rich atmospheres. They also have enlarged, external sensory organs at the base of their skulls that provides them with extrasensory abilities.

## A DIRECTOR'S FAVORITE (cont'd)

Dee Baker, who does the voices for the clones, made what Filoni considered a very good attempt—but Filoni kept tinkering, and eventually turned to another movie for inspiration. Filoni says he was a huge fan of *The Lord of the Rings* as a child, and loved Ian McKellen's portrayal of Gandalf in Peter Jackson's movies. So he asked James Arnold Taylor if he could try a voice with similar tonal qualities as McKellen. Taylor did so, and after all that work, Plo Koon's dialogue was complete in about fifteen minutes.

## SPACE BATTLE

In "Rising *Malevolence*," we see Plo Koon fight with both bravery and brains, such as in the "alley-oop play" that flings the clone trooper Boost behind the attacking droids so he can fire at them. But in discussing that action sequence, George Lucas had a question: Could Plo Koon really survive in space?

"To me it makes a lot of sense," Dave Filoni says. "He's an alien. I don't know what he can and can't do—it's not defined. So if we say he can go out into space, then he can go out into space."

Lucas eventually let Filoni have his way, but insisted that the script include Plo telling his clones that he could survive outside "for a brief time." And he teased Filoni that he'd managed to make six *Star Wars* movies without anybody fighting in space. In fact, "Destroy *Malevolence*" originally was going to include a lightsaber fight between Plo Koon and General Grievous on the exterior of the *Malevolence*, with Plo Koon wearing a new breath mask modeled after that of the clone troopers and featuring the classic "stormtrooper frown." The mask was mocked up as a maquette but didn't get used, Filoni says. As for Plo Koon's lightsaber skills, they'll be on display in a later episode—and Filoni says it will be the kind of fight "that I know the fans want and are asking for."

As for Plo Koon's trip into space, Filoni says, "I think it builds his character because he's doing it for his men. What he's saying is 'I can survive for a brief time and it's going to keep you guys alive.' And that's the important thing to take home."

## General Grievous

Commander of the Separatist droid armies, the ruthless cyborg General Grievous is a highly-skilled warlord with a personal vendetta against the Jedi Order.

## EPISODE HIGHLIGHT

NOW THE REPUBLIC WILL LEARN OF OUR ION CANNON.

YOUR FAILURE IS MOST UNFORTUNATE.

I'LL NEED TO DISCUSS THIS WITH MY MASTER.

## NEVER CRY WOLFFE

Briefly glimpsed in "Rising *Malevolence*" are the wolf-like markings on the armor of the clones serving Plo Koon and Commander Wolffe.

The design's origin? Simple: "I like wolves," Filoni says. The director says he was a fan of the movie *Never Cry Wolf* as a child, has traveled into the Arctic to see wolves in the wild, and is keenly interested in tough questions about how to balance the needs of ranchers with those of wolves.

In a future episode, Filoni promises, we'll see Wolffe and his "wolf pack" again.

The clone suffers an injury between "Rising *Malevolence*" and his next appearance, winding up with a scar across his face and a cybernetic silver eye. (Besides giving the clone a rakish look, the injury will make it easier to tell him apart from all the other identical faces.) His helmet will have a wolf design painted on it, and a silver visor so he's looking out through the wolf's eyes.

"You see he's the leader of the wolf pack," Filoni says. "I'm going to get that in the series at some point."

## Clone Commander Wolffe

Wolffe is a veteran clone trooper commander serving onboard the *Venator*-class Star Destroyer *Triumphant* under Jedi General Plo Koon.

# GALACTIC DISPATCHES
## THE SEPARATIST SUPERWEAPON

Among the Separatists' greatest allies are the Quarren, who share a planet with the Mon Calamari but have disagreed with their neighbors about nearly everything for thousands of years. While the Mon Cals (as the Quarren call them) supported the Republic, many of the squid-faced Quarren sided with the Confederacy of Independent Systems, and offered the Separatists their skills as shipwrights.

The most valuable Separatist shipyard was Pammant, in the Calamari sector. There, the Quarren Free Dac Volunteers Engineering Corps built kilometer-long *Providence*-class destroyers for the Separatists. Three of those great ships— the *Invisible Hand*, *Lucid Voice*, and the *Colicoid Swarm*— would strike fear in hearts on many Republic worlds during the Clone Wars.

Bad enough. But Republic spies watching Pammant worried about what was happening in a huge, heavily guarded dry dock that even their best operatives couldn't sneak into. That dry dock was the birthplace of the *Malevolence*, a *Subjugator*-class heavy cruiser with two massive ion pulse cannons whose blasts could disable any ship.

When the massive *Malevolence* finally lumbered out of dry dock, the spies rushed frantically to report to Coruscant—but were captured by Separatist agents who had been watching them the whole time. The *Malevolence's* secret was safe, and her ion cannons would leave a trail of shattered ships from the Core to the Mid Rim as the Jedi tried to track her down. And if the watchers had waited a few weeks longer, they would have seen a second heavy cruiser fire up its engines. This was the *Malevolence's* sister ship, the *Devastation*.

## Episode 3:

DOES ANYONE CARE WHAT THE PADAWAN THINKS?

**Original Airdate:** 10/10/08

**Written by** Stephen Melching

**Directed by** Brian Kalin O'Connell

**Cast**
Matt Lanter:
    Anakin Skywalker
Ashley Eckstein:
    Ahsoka Tano
Tom Kane:
    Admiral Yularen, narrator
James Arnold Taylor:
    Obi-Wan Kenobi, Plo Koon
Dee Bradley Baker:
    Clone troopers
Matthew Wood:
    General Grievous, battle
    droids
Corey Burton:
    Count Dooku
Gwendoline Yeo:
    Nala Se

**Location:** Balmorra Run

# SHADOW OF MALEVOLENCE

"Easy is the path to wisdom for those not blinded by themselves."

## SYNOPSIS

General Grievous and the *Malevolence* make their way towards a Republic medical station. Anakin leads a squadron of Y-wing fighters to stop the battleship. He thinks that a team of small starfighters could out maneuver the ships's ion cannon. Anakin leads the ship through a giant neebray-infested shortcut and beats Grievous to the station. The Y-wings attack the *Malevolence*'s ion cannon, causing it to backfire and disable the ship's hyperdrive.

MASTER SKYWALKER SEEMS TO INSPIRE GREAT CONFIDENCE IN HIS MEN.

HE DOES LEAD BY EXAMPLE.

## NEWSREEL

A deadly weapon unleashed! The Separatist battleship *Malevolence* advances unopposed through Republic space, tearing apart any ship that stands in its path. After a daring rescue and narrow escape, Anakin Skywalker prepares a counterattack on the enemy and its diabolical droid commander, General Grievous.... ∎

**Vehicles:** *Resolute* (*Venator*-class Star Destroyer), *Negotiator* (*Venator*-class Star Destroyer), Separatist boarding craft, Kaliida Shoals Medical Center, Plo Koon's Delta-7B *Aethersprite*-class starfighter, BTL-B Y-wing starfighter, Republic medical frigate, *Malevolence* (*Subjugator*-type heavy cruiser), Republic attack gunship, pod hunter

**Weapons:** ion cannon, lightsaber, proton torpedo

## JOY IN REPETITION

A number of things in "Shadow of *Malevolence*" evoke "classic" *Star Wars*, from the Y-wings and their attack run on the *Malevolence* to the shot of battle droids cringing away from the giant ship's ion cannon, just as the Death Star troopers ducked when the original Death Star's superlaser fired.

As Henry Gilroy explains, he and Dave Filoni were careful to walk a fine line between nods to the past and repeating things too much.

"Whenever we got too close to repeating things from the films, George would tell us, 'I already did that,'" he recalls.

## CHARACTERS

Trooper Boost
Count Dooku
General Grievous
Obi-Wan Kenobi
Plo Koon
Chancellor Palpatine
R2-D2
R7-D4
Nala Se
Anakin Skywalker
Ahsoka Tano
Mace Windu
Commander Wolffe
Yoda
Admiral Wullf Yularen

## Anakin Skywalker

As a General in the Grand Army of the Republic, Jedi Knight Anakin Skywalker commands the Star Destroyer *Resolute*.

## ALIEN PROFILE

### Kaminoans

Kaminoans are a highly intelligent species from the water-covered world of Kamino, which lies deep in the area known as Wild Space—far beyond the Outer Rim Territories. The Kaminoans are tall, thin beings with pale skin and small heads that sit atop long necks. Because of the Kaminoan's exceptional cloning technology, they were the perfect choice to create the Republic's clone army.

## EPISODE HIGHLIGHT

TORPEDOES AWAY!

## JOY IN REPETITION (cont'd)

"We really strived to create story elements that didn't repeat the films, but were 'in the spirit' of the films. George told me several times that he wanted the effervescent, fun quality of *A New Hope* in *The Clone Wars*. That meant it had to be humorous, thrilling, scary, amazing, etc.—my job was to come up with new ways to bring back the sense of wonder the films created."

Yes, Gilroy says, the Y-wing assault on the *Malevolence* has several lines of dialogue that are right out of the Death Star attack. "It makes sense because the participants in a military attack always say the same things," he says. "For example in a traditional war movie, you'll hear, 'Target is in range. Open the bomb bay doors. Bombs away.' In *Star Wars*, characters say, 'Shields double-front. Watch out for those fighters. Stay on target.' It's the same thing."

TARGET THOSE ESCAPE PODS, I HAVE A REPUTATION TO UPHOLD.

## AN OLD DESIGN'S SECOND CHANCE

"We wanted to have a *Bismarck*-style battleship," Dave Filoni says of General Grievous's terrible warship *Malevolence*. "We wanted this massive weapon that the Republic wasn't aware of—it was a mystery, it was wiping out people, and no one knew what it was because there were no survivors. That's always a good way to start off."

The design for the *Malevolence* dates back to a Separatist communications ship imagined but not used for Episode III. But Filoni notes that the Episode III design "didn't quite look like what we considered a *Star Wars* ship to look like."

Filoni started talking with Russell Chong, who's studied Ralph McQuarrie's classic *Star Wars* designs, and thinking about the Separatists and where they fit in with the saga's history.

Filoni calls the Separatists "odd villains—they're against the Jedi, but they're kind of right in that the Senate's corrupt and a Sith Lord's running it and the Republic's falling apart." Moreover, the Republic forces become the Imperials seen in the classic trilogy, with the clone troopers becoming stormtroopers and the wedge-shaped Jedi Cruisers giving way to the Empire's triangular Star Destroyers.

## Nala Se

Nala Se is a Kaminoan who works at Kaliida Shoals Medical Center and tends to injured clone troopers.

## VEHICLE PROFILE

### Plo Koon's Delta-7B *Aethersprite*-class light interceptor

**Model:** Delta-7B *Aethersprite*-class light interceptor

**Class:** Starfighter

**Weapons:**
• Laser cannons

## TRIVIA

These four-legged power droids are called plunk droids after the sound that they make.

## AN OLD DESIGN'S SECOND CHANCE (cont'd)

Given all that, Filoni had a suggestion: "Why don't we look at the Mon Calamari cruiser and the Rebel transport and use that kind of shell shape to get the *Malevolence* more in line with classic *Star Wars*?"

The Banking Clan frigate already had such a shell shape. But the *Malevolence* is also a superweapon akin to the Death Star. So within the shell shape of the *Malevolence* is a jagged city of sorts, which recalls the half-completed Death Star seen in *Return of the Jedi*.

## BIRTH OF THE Y-WING

In "Shadow of *Malevolence*," Anakin, Ahsoka, and the clone pilots of Shadow Squadron travel along the Balmorra Run through the dangerous Kaliida Nebula to intercept the *Malevolence* before it can lay waste to the Kaliida Shoals Medical Center and its thousands of injured clones. The starfighters they choose are a familiar sight to *Star Wars* fans— a variation of the Y-wing fighter first seen attacking the Death Star in *A New Hope*.

For Dave Filoni, the Y-wing began with a childhood memory of a repurposed fighter stripped of its coverings and rebuilt by Rebel technicians. Filoni recalls thinking, "Hmm, I guess that means the Rebel Alliance actually inherited a bunch of equipment from the Clone War that Obi-Wan Kenobi had talked about and they were using it. But they were using, for whatever reason, the beat-up stuff." (His memory is accurate—that explanation is found in 1977's *The Star Wars Sketchbook*, by Joe Johnston.)

### ALIEN PROFILE
#### Neebrays

These great winged creatures are known in many parts of the galaxy, riding the solar winds along ancient migration routes in pods of adults and juveniles. They feed on the organic compounds within nebulae, and are generally found within these great clouds of gas and dust. But neebray have a complex lifecycle that xenobiologists are still studying. Newborn neebray, some no bigger than a human child's finger, are often found in the atmospheres of planets, where they feed on sunlight and atmospheric gases. Juveniles sometimes attach themselves to starships entering or leaving the atmosphere, but have also been found in deep space, apparently hibernating.

## R7-D4
Jedi Master Plo Koon's battle worn astromech droid and copilot of his Delta-7B *Aethersprite*-class light interceptor.

## EPISODE HIGHLIGHT

BROADSIDE, IF WE MAKE IT THROUGH THIS ONE, DRINKS ARE ON ME.

IF ANYTHING, IT IS SKYWALKER WHO WILL UNDERESTIMATE THIS SHIP AND ITS POWER.

I CAN ALREADY TASTE IT.

## BIRTH OF THE Y-WING (cont'd)

The Y-wing we see in "Shadow of *Malevolence*" fits with Johnston's explanation—it has smooth hull plating covering its engines and its fuselage, and a bubble canopy first seen in an old Ralph McQuarrie concept painting of the fighter.

"It's just a real thrill to have a squadron of clone pilots led by Anakin Skywalker fighting in the Clone Wars," Filoni says. "As a *Star Wars* fan, that's a pretty romantic notion."

## Matchstick

Y-wing clone pilot in Shadow Squadron with the designation Shadow 2. He is one of several clone pilots to die in the Battle of the Kaliida Nebula.

# GALACTIC DISPATCHES
## THE BALMORRA RUN

As a child, Anakin Skywalker loved to hang around Mos Espa's cantinas, listening to spacers tell tall tales—as well as the occasional true story. The freighter jocks felt sorry for the young slave who wanted to know about star systems he'd probably never see.

One story Anakin heard was about the Balmorra Run, a hair-raising shortcut smugglers used to avoid customs checkpoints when flying from the sleazy spaceport of Trigalis to the law-abiding worlds of the Chommel sector. The run—named because it was charted by a gang of smugglers from Balmorra—twisted around star clusters before knifing through the Kaliida Nebula, a churning cloud of gas and dust lit from within by newborn stars. The run had to be flown old-style, by relying on eyes and reflexes—the way it must have been before pilot droids and navicomputers took all the fun out of space travel.

Years later, when General Grievous threatened the Kaliida Medical Center, Anakin remembered those stories. Shooting the Balmorra Run in the Republic's new Y-wing fighters would let him and Shadow Squadron beat the *Malevolence* to Kaliida Shoals, and show once again that a former Tatooine slave could outfly anybody.

But Anakin had either forgotten or had never heard about one of the run's dangers. As Plo Koon knew all too well, the Kaliida Nebula was also a neebray nesting ground—and with instruments all but useless, even an expert pilot could run smack into one of the great gas gulpers.

# Episode 4:

WE'RE DOOMED.

**Original Airdate:** 10/17/08

**Written by** Tim Burns

**Directed by** Brian Kalin O'Connell

**Cast**
Matt Lanter:
    Anakin Skywalker
James Arnold Taylor:
    Obi-Wan Kenobi, Plo Koon
Catherine Taber:
    Padmé Amidala
Matthew Wood:
    General Grievous, battle
    droids
Anthony Daniels:
    C-3PO
Ashley Eckstein:
    Ahsoka Tano
Dee Bradley Baker:
    Clone troopers
Tom Kane:
    Admiral Yularen, narrator
Corey Burton:
    Count Dooku
Olivia d'Abo:
    Luminara Unduli

# DESTROY MALEVOLENCE

"A plan is only as good as those who see it through."

## SYNOPSIS

Republic cruisers continue to attack the damaged *Malevolence* as Senator Padmé Amidala's ship drops out of hyperdrive right next to the battleship. By the time that she realizes that she's been tricked, her ship has been caught in the *Malevolence*'s tractor beam. Anakin and Obi-Wan head toward the *Malevolence* to rescue her. Aboard the ship, they get separated and Obi-Wan battles Grievous as Anakin and Padmé sabotage the ship's navigation computer. The Jedi and Padmé escape the *Malevolence*, and Grievous chases after them in his starfighter. The *Malevolence* attempts to make the jump to hyperspace, but the coordinates that Anakin programmed into the navigation computer send it crashing into a dead moon instead.

## NEWSREEL

Grievous in retreat! Before the battleship *Malevolence* could destroy an Outer Rim clone medical base, a Republic strike force, under the command of Jedi General Anakin Skywalker, crippled the warship, disabling its dreaded ion cannon. Now the Jedi relentlessly pursue the *Malevolence*.... ■

**Location:** Outer Rim

**Vehicles:** Grievous's *Soulless One* (Belbullab-22 starfighter), *Twilight* (G9 Rigger), *Resolute* (*Venator*-class Star Destroyer), V-19 torrent starfighter, *Malevolence* (*Subjugator*-type heavy cruiser), Republic attack gunship, Naboo Yacht

**Weapons:** E-5 blaster rifle, ELG-3A blaster pistol, lightsaber

## CHARACTERS

Senator Padmé Amidala
C-3PO
Commander Cody
Count Dooku
General Grievous
Obi-Wan Kenobi
Plo Koon
R2-D2
Anakin Skywalker
Ahsoka Tano
Luminara Unduli
Admiral Wullf Yularen

## ROGER, ROGER

One difference between *The Clone Wars* and the prequels is that the battle droids have traded the occasional squeal or dimwitted "roger, roger" for jokey lines and slapstick moments. "The comedy aspect of the battle droids was all George," says Henry Gilroy. "He enjoys the old *Keystone Cops* silent comedies, and the droid humor is inspired by their slapstick antics."

But that humor has a purpose, he notes: "I believe Dave and I were showing George our first animatic cut of the *Clone Wars* film, which began with the opening assault on the Teth monastery.

## Senator Padmé Amidala

Padmé Amidala serves as the Senator of Naboo, taking the position once occupied by Palpatine. In a galaxy undergoing tumultuous changes, her outspoken nature has shone as a beacon of reason and rationality in an increasingly fragmented Senate.

## DROID PROFILE
### Protocol Droid

A droid whose primary purpose is to aid and assist diplomats and high-level figures. Their programming includes languages, cultures, and diplomacy. Common models are the TC and 3PO series. They were programmed with personalities, emotions, and the ability to learn and grow very similar to organic beings. The 3PO units are fluent in over six million languages.

## VEHICLE PROFILE
### *Soulless One*

**Class:** Belbullab-22 starfighter

**Weapons:**
• Two triple laser cannons

**ROGER, ROGER (cont'd)**

It was deadly serious, with clones getting blasted and this 14-year-old girl, Ahsoka, being exposed to the grim reality of war. George stopped us and said, 'You guys are taking this too seriously.' And he went back and started adding in the comedy bits with the droids. When it was all cut together, the battle became swashbuckling fun, as opposed to intense life and death. From then on, Dave and I would look for where to add 'droid humor' to lighten the tone—but it was George who most often put the droid jokes in."

## THE *STAR WARS* RAILWAY

A startling feature of the *Malevolence* is the train tracks going back and forth across its vast interior—tracks with speeding trains that are ridden—on purpose and by accident—by Anakin, Padme, Obi-Wan, Grievous, and C-3PO.

"That was one of the times where I kind of let the layout department go with it," Filoni says. He thought trains made sense for carrying battle droids from one end of the Separatists' mile-long superweapon to the other, and had pictured a couple of tube tunnels. Instead, Filoni recalls, he got "this immense interior with all these tracks—this giant chasm in the ship. And I was like, 'Wow, that's more than I thought it was going to be.' But it was cool."

Filoni says he grew up knowing something about trains because his brother Mike is a huge train enthusiast. (In fact, he now works on a railway.) "So I thought it was funny there were trains in *Star Wars* now," Filoni says. "It's kind of my fault."

## B1 Battle Droid

The B1 battle droids serve as the main infantry of the Separatist Alliance. While they are not the most intelligent droids, they are unquestioningly loyal and fearless.

## WEAPON PROFILE

### ELG-3A Blaster Pistol

This compact blaster is standard issue on all Naboo royal cruisers and battleships.

## EPISODE HIGHLIGHT

GENERAL KENOBI, DID YOU REALLY THINK THAT I'D LEAVE THE HYPERDRIVE UNPROTECTED?

ANYTHING IS POSSIBLE . . .

YOU HAVEN'T EXACTLY IMPRESSED ME TODAY.

## THE *STAR WARS* RAILWAY (cont'd)

When Grievous's train comes to a halt, an automated voice politely tells him to "mind the gap"—a message heard over and over again by riders of the London Underground, better known as the Tube. That was a contribution by Skywalker Sound's Matt Wood, who's also the voice of Grievous. Filoni suggested that Wood act like a station conductor, and Wood did the rest.

According to Filoni, the sound room is where any number of ad-libs are born. For instance, in *The Clone Wars* movie, a battle droid tells Asajj Ventress that Count Dooku wants a report, and the annoyed Dark Jedi hurls the poor machine off a cliff. "We had thrown so many battle droids off the cliff at that point that we were almost like, 'This is ridiculous,'"

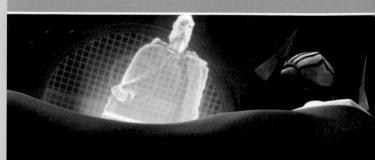

Filoni recalls. "So I said, 'Have this one go "Why?"'" Like he finally realizes that something horrible's happening to him."

"Sometimes you're tired and it seems funnier than maybe it is," Filoni says. "But there are a lot of fun things Matt and the guys do in sound."

## ALL TOGETHER NOW

"Destroy *Malevolence*" concludes with an image of Anakin, Obi-Wan, Padmé, C-3PO, and R2-D2 standing together—an instantly iconic shot Filoni calls "a classic callback to the way *Star Wars* films end. They always end with this silent series of images, and then almost a portrait shot. There are many different ways to do it, and George has done a lot of them." That closing shot isn't unique to "Destroy *Malevolence*"— it's echoed in an episode earlier, at

## C-3PO

Senator Amidala's personal protocol droid. He is fluent in over six million forms of communication.

I DO BELIEVE I'M LOST IN ENEMY TERRITORY. AND ALL ALONE.

DON'T SHOOT, I SURRENDER.

R2-D2, OH MY, YOU ARE A SIGHT FOR SORE CIRCUITS.

MASTER ANAKIN SENT YOU TO FIND ME? WHAT KEPT YOU THEN?

BEEPOOP

**TRIVIA**

The Naboo yacht is an H-type Nubian yacht, which was created by the Nubian Design Collective, and then customized by the Theed Palace Space Vessel Engineering Corps for Senator Padmé Amidala's personal use.

> THERE HE GOES AGAIN, CRAVING ADVENTURE AND EXCITEMENT.

> YOU GET USED TO IT.

## Admiral Wullf Yularen

Admiral in the Republic Navy under the command of Jedi General Anakin Skywalker, he serves aboard the Star Destroyer *Resolute*.

## ALL TOGETHER NOW (cont'd)

the conclusion of "Shadow of *Malevolence*."

"The last shot is Anakin and Ahsoka standing in a hanger together with Artoo there, and some Y-wings fly by," Filoni says. "That's pretty much the end of *The Empire Strikes Back*, when Luke and Leia are in the medical frigate."

Such classic shots connect us visually to *Star Wars*, Filoni says. But they're not easy to make happen. Take "Destroy *Malevolence*," for instance—"it's a very rare opportunity in *The Clone Wars* to have Padme, Anakin, Obi-Wan, Artoo, and Threepio—I mean, when are they ever all together? You have no idea how hard it is to get Artoo and Threepio in the same place."

But Filoni is determined to find chances: "When you have the opportunity, it's the best way to end a *Star Wars* anything— with that group portrait of the heroes, and a snapshot of what they've gone through."

# GALACTIC DISPATCHES
## THE TROUBLE WITH BATTLE DROIDS

The first B1 battle droids to roll off Baktoid Combat Automata's assembly lines were designed not for war, but for defending Trade Federation transports against space pirates and bandits. Baktoid gradually made improvements to these battle droids, beginning by giving them improved combat modules, but plenty of the original B1s remained in service throughout the Clone Wars.

At the Battle of Naboo, the Trade Federation's droid army shut down when young Anakin Skywalker destroyed the orbiting droid control ship. Disgusted by the sight of Gungans kicking over motionless battle droids, the Federation retrofitted many first-generation B1s with cognitive modules allowing independent thought. This prevented remote shutdowns and let the Separatists teach the droids new things by uploading new programming to their "brains." Since Separatist warships had few flesh-and-blood crewmembers, many B1s were programmed to serve as pilots, gunners, and even as emergency responders.

But the B1s—particularly the oldest models—were being pushed to the limits of their original programming. They could now perform specialized tasks and even learn, but they couldn't do either very well—and later, more powerful cognitive modules were saved for the Separatists' newer war droids. As the Separatists cut back on maintenance, many early B1s' cognitive modules suffered data corruption and system errors, leading to shutdowns or behavioral anomalies. And older B1s that kept working sometimes became "chatty," offering running commentaries on their situations as their modules struggled to process data overflows.

# Episode 5:

LOOKS LIKE WE GOT OURSELVES A BATCH OF SHINIES.

# ROOKIES

"The best confidence builder is experience."

## SYNOPSIS

Clone officers Commander Cody and Captain Rex are sent to inspect the remote Rishi outpost in the Outer Rim. The outpost is responsible for protecting the cloning facilities on Kamino. However, the outpost has been overrun with droid commandos, leaving only a handful of rookie clones left. Rex and Cody take command of these rookies and lead them on a daring mission to destroy the outpost and alert the Republic of the imminent attack on Kamino.

**Original Airdate:** 10/24/08

**Written by** Stephen Melching

**Directed by** Justin Ridge

**Cast**
Dee Bradley Baker:
    Clone troopers
James Arnold Taylor:
    Obi-Wan Kenobi
Matthew Wood:
    General Grievous, battle
    droids
Matt Lanter:
    Anakin Skywalker
Tom Kane:
    Admiral Yularen, narrator
Nika Futterman:
    Asajj Ventress
Gwendoline Yeo:
    Hologram VJ

**Location:** Rishi system

I SHOULDN'T HAVE TO REMIND YOU THAT THIS QUADRANT IS KEY TO THE OUTER RIM. IF THE DROIDS GET PAST THIS STATION, THEY CAN SURPRISE ATTACK THE FACILITIES WHERE WE WERE BORN ON OUR HOMEWORLD OF KAMINO.

## NEWSREEL

Clone forces rally! As the war escalates in the Outer Rim, the Jedi Knights are spread thinly across the galaxy. Many now clones are rushed into service to support their Jedi generals. Unfortunately, because of the relentless demands of battle, many young clones must join the struggle before their intensive training has been completed. These clones, manning a vital network of tracking stations, are all that stand between the Republic and invasion.... ■

**Vehicles:** *Consular*-class space cruiser, Republic frigate, V-19 Torrent starfighter, *Resolute* (*Venator*-class Star Destroyer), *Obex* (*Nu-class* attack shuttle), *Lucrehulk*-class battleship, C-9979 landing craft

**Weapons:** DC-17 blaster, DC-15A blaster rifle, D-15S blaster, E-5 blaster rifle, thermal detonator, Z-6 rotary blaster cannon, droid commando vibrosword, stun baton

## A BATCHER'S LIFE

For fans of the new series, "Rookies" was a bit of a change of pace—an episode that gives us only brief glimpses of the series' major characters, and keeps them on the sidelines while the action unfolds.

In the "classic" *Star Wars* movies, the Empire's stormtroopers were cannon fodder— one of their only hints of individuality

## CHARACTERS

Commander Cody
Trooper Cutup
Trooper Fives
Droid commandos
Trooper Droidbait
Trooper Echo
General Grievous
Trooper Hevy
Hologram VJ
Obi-Wan Kenobi
Trooper Nub
Sergeant O'Niner
R2-D2
Captain Rex
Anakin Skywalker
Asajj Ventress
Admiral Wullf Yularen

# Commander Cody

Commander of the the 212th Attack Battalion, Cody often serves alongside Jedi General Obi-Wan Kenobi.

## PROFILE

### Clone Troopers

Identical soldiers created on the world of Kamino using the genetic template of Mandalorian bounty hunter Jango Fett.

## EPISODE HIGHLIGHT

THEY SHOULD HAVE CHECKED IN FROM THE RISHI STATION HOURS AGO.

IT APPEARS YOUR CAPTAIN FOLLOWS ORDERS AS WELL AS YOU DO.

HMM. PERHAPS CODY IS BORING REX WITH STANDARD PROCEDURES AND PROTOCOL.

## A BATCHER'S LIFE (cont'd)

(not counting wails as they fall into apparently bottomless canyons) is the snippet of Death Star gossip overhead by Ben Kenobi as he steals away from his sabotage of the tractor beam in "A New Hope." But in *The Clone Wars* we see the galaxy's troopers in a different light. They may all be clones and wear interchangeable armor, but behind those identical helmets are young men with different personalities and hopes and dreams.

"We were a dozen scripts into the series and George came in one day and said, 'Do a story with only clones,'" Henry Gilroy recalls. "Dave and I were excited because it was a chance to explore the different points of view the clones could have. For example, Echo is kind of the nerdy, by-the-book soldier, where Hevy is unfulfilled and wants to be out fighting on the front lines.

Dee Bradley Baker—who does the voices of the clones—did and does a terrific job bringing all the varying personalities to life."

Gilroy says to make sure an episode using new characters grabs the audience, "it helps to put them in situations that are universally

relatable. Just about everyone has been in a situation where they are inexperienced or new at something and get in over their heads. These clones are brand-new soldiers who totally get their butts kicked—yet prove that with some veteran leadership and some tough resolve they can turn it around and be very effective."

## BUILDING A BETTER B1

"Rookies" marks the debut of the Separatists' commando droids—battle droids that are far

## Commando Droids
Elite battle droids created for stealth assignments.

## VEHICLE PROFILE
### *Obex*

**Model:** *Nu*-class attack shuttle

**Class:** Shuttle

**Weapons:**
- Medium laser cannons
- Double light laser cannon

## WEAPON PROFILE
### Thermal Detonator

A small, handheld explosive device

## ALIEN PROFILE
### Rishi Eels

A large, carnivorous moraylike creature native to the Rishi moon. It is capable of eating a person whole.

## WEAPON PROFILE

### DC-15A blaster rifle

A more powerful, long-ranging version of the DC-15S blaster

## BUILDING A BETTER B1 (cont'd)

greater threats than the familiar B1s dismissed by clone troopers as mere "clankers."

"As the war intensifies and as the stories develop, the Separatists had to develop more threatening droids so that they could compete with the Jedi and the clones, who are much better warriors than the battle droids ever could be," Dave Filoni explains. "The commando droids were definitely a reaction story wise by us," after

ROGER. ROGER.

audiences had become used to comically inept battle droids.

"We wanted them to be a real threat," Filoni says. "We wanted to know there was peril for the clones and for the Jedi when these guys were around. So their proportions are more human. They can talk and change their voice. They're obviously more intelligent. They're substantially faster than a regular battle droid. And thus they become a real threat."

Which, for him, raises a question: Why don't the Separatists just use hundreds of thousands of commando droids and win the war against the Republic rather easily?

"For a guy like Nute Gunray it comes down to cost," Filoni surmises. "Obviously a more sophisticated

### Hevy

A clone trooper assigned to the Rishi outpost, he has an affection for large weapons and valiantly sacrifices himself to save his fellow clones.

**EPISODE HIGHLIGHT**

## WEAPON PROFILE

### DC-17
### Hand Blaster

A heavy blaster pistol used by clone captains and commanders

> TODAY WE FIGHT FOR MORE THAN THE REPUBLIC, TODAY WE FIGHT FOR ALL OUR BROTHERS BACK HOME.

## BUILDING A BETTER B1 (cont'd)

droid is more expensive to make. It's harder to manufacture. The raw materials aren't as easy to get. So you have these really massively produced dimwitted droids and the less-produced commando droids. That's one of the reasons they're more valuable."

Still, Filoni says, give the B1s their due: "The base gets taken over twice—once by the commando droids and once by an entire squad of regular battle droids. So it shows you that while dimwitted, the regular battle droids are still a threat."

## Sergeant O-Niner

Commanding officer of the Rishi base, Sergeant O-Niner understands the importance of their assignment, and takes his responsibilities seriously.

# GALACTIC DISPATCHES
## THE ROAD TO KAMINO

Kamino is the closest thing to home the clone troopers have—it's where the Kaminoans took Jango Fett's genetic material and duplicated it in countless vats to create an army for the Republic.

The waterworld sits "above" the galactic plane on the fringes of the Rishi Maze, a dwarf satellite galaxy. The market for Kamino clones dried up centuries before the Clone Wars, and in the years before the Battle of Geonosis the system was quietly removed from most star charts under mysterious circumstances. But Wild Space's small-time traders and smugglers remembered it, and Obi-Wan Kenobi's old friend Dexter Jettster was able to guide him to the planet the Jedi archivists had forgotten.

Ending clone production on Kamino could tip the balance of the war, so the Republic set up listening posts to defend it against a Separatist attack. One of those posts was located on the Rishi moon, orbiting the planet of the same name at the start of the little-trafficked trade route known as the Zareca String. The string was the only reliable hyperspace route to the Rishi Maze—from Rishi, it led "up" out of the main galaxy, connecting bleak systems used by traders and scouts to refuel, recheck navigation, and restock supplies.

Each system in the string had its own listening post staffed by bored clones. But compared to their colleagues located farther along the string, Rishi Station's rookies actually had it good—at least their post had air.

# Episode 6:

> YOU'LL BE SORRY YOU EVER CAME ABOARD MY SHIP, JEDI.

**Original Airdate:** 11/7/08

**Written by** George Krstic

**Directed by** Rob Coleman

**Cast**
Matt Lanter:
    Anakin Skywalker
Ashley Eckstein:
    Ahsoka Tano
Matthew Wood:
    General Grievous, battle
    droids
Ron Perlman:
    Gha Nachkt
James Arnold Taylor:
    Obi-Wan Kenobi
Dee Bradley Baker:
    Clone troopers
Tom Kane:
    Admiral Yularen, narrator

**Location:** Bothan Sector

# DOWNFALL OF A DROID

"Trust in your friends, and they'll have reason to trust in you."

## SYNOPSIS

Anakin executes a daring ambush on General Grievous's fleet, but suffers serious damage to his starfighter. When he wakes up in the medical bay, he's informed by Ahsoka that R2-D2 was lost in the battle. Obi-Wan Kenobi, concerned that R2-D2's memory contains Republic secrets, sends Anakin to find the droid. However, Anakin's new astromech droid, R3-S6, apparently malfunctions and almost delivers the Jedi into the waiting hands of Grievous.

> MASTER, THEY JUST DELIVERED YOUR NEW ASTROMECH DROID. THIS IS R3-S6.

# NEWSREEL

After suffering a series of disastrous defeats at the hands of General Grievous, the Republic's foothold in the Outer Rim is in jeopardy. Commissioned to protect the strategic world of Bothawui, Anakin Skywalker and his weary battle group are all that stands between the system and domination by the droid army.... ∎

**Vehicles:** Grievous's *Soulless One* (Belbullab-22 starfighter), *Twilight* (G9 Rigger), *Resolute* (*Venator*-class Star Destroyer), V-19 torrent starfighter, *Munificent*-class star frigate, Anakin Skywalker's Delta-7B *Aethersprite*-class starfighter, *Vulture's Claw* (Trandoshan scavenger ship), All Terrain Tactical Enforcer (AT-TE), vulture droid starfighter

**Weapons:** Lightsaber, restraining bolt, E-5 droid blasters

## CHARACTERS

General Grievous
Obi-Wan Kenobi
Gha Nachkt
R2-D2
R3-S6 ("Goldie")
Captain Rex
Anakin Skywalker
Ahsoka Tano
Admiral Wullf Yularen

## GOLDIE'S SECRET

The black and gold coloration of R3-S6 was Dave Filoni's choice. The supervising director is from Pittsburgh, whose professional sports teams—the Pirates, Steelers, and Penguins—all wear black and gold.

"It's just a little nod to my hometown to have an astromech in there that's black and gold," Filoni says. "It's too bad he turns out to be a villain."

Filoni is aware that the city fathers see an insult hiding in the fact that Goldie is a bad guy. But Filoni swears he's a loyal native son: "It's not a statement about Pittsburgh at all. I love Pittsburgh."

# R2-D2

A spunky, independent astromech, R2-D2 serves Anakin Skywalker. His barrel-shaped body hides a huge number of tools, including a holoprojector and a computer interface.

I AM EN ROUTE TO THE RENDEZVOUS POINT, GENERAL. I HAVE GOT THE MERCHANDISE YOU ARE LOOKING FOR.

## ALIEN PROFILE

### Trandoshans

Burly reptilians from the same star system as the Wookiees, Trandoshans are known for their great strength and ability to regenerate lost limbs. Many Trandoshans serve as bounty hunters or slavers.

## NOT ALL LIZARDS ARE ALIKE

*Star Wars* fans first met a lizard-like Trandoshan in *The Empire Strikes Back*, when they spied the bounty hunter Bossk on the bridge of Darth Vader's Super Star Destroyer. Bossk got a sneak-preview action figure from Kenner, but he doesn't have much to do in the movie—he bends a toe over a ledge, grumbles something at Admiral Piett, and that's a wrap. (Granted, this is more than any bounty hunter other than Boba Fett gets to do in the short scene.)

"A great opportunity in doing *The Clone Wars* and expanding the *Star Wars* universe was to see one of these lizards do something for a change,"

## VEHICLE PROFILE

### V-19 Torrent starfighter

**Model:** V-19 Torrent starfighter

**Class:** Starfighter

**Weapons:**
- Blaster cannons
- Concussion missile launchers

I THINK STUBBY IS DEFECTIVE.

Dave Filoni says. "Let's watch them run around."

In the Expanded Universe we see more of Bossk and even meet his father, Cradossk. And the two do occasionally run around. But nothing learned in these meetings is terribly surprising: Trandoshans are vicious lizards who are very strong, dislike the Wookiees with whom they share a star system, can regenerate limbs even after they're pulled out of their sockets (by an angry Wookiee, for instance) and make great bounty hunters.

## PLANET PROFILE
### Bothawui

**Region:** Mid Rim

Bothawui is the home of the Bothans, master spies and information gatherers who are suspicious of other species and see politics as a ruthless game to be played with no letup and no mercy.

## EPISODE HIGHLIGHT

UGH. WHAT'S THAT SMELL?

YOU'LL GET USED TO IT.

## Gha Nachkt

A Trandoshan scavenger who scours through the debris left in the aftermath of space battles during the Clone Wars in his freighter *Vulture's Claw*. An unscrupulous trader, he sells his salvage to the highest bidder.

SUICIDE IS NOT THE JEDI WAY, MASTER.

YOU SHOULD LISTEN TO YOUR PADAWAN.

AS YOU LISTENED TO YOURS, MY OLD MASTER?

On the *Resolute*, Ahsoka's tactical readout says in Aurebesh: ATTE RUL3Z TAKE THAT GRIEVOUS.

## NOT ALL LIZARDS ARE ALIKE (cont'd)

But are they all like that? Not at all, as Filoni shows by introducing us to the rumpled, roly-poly Trandoshan scavenger Gha Nachkt, who gave the director another chance to show *Star Wars* fans that not all members of a species look and act the same.

"You go outside and all of us human beings are different," he says. "Some are fatter, some are thinner, some are taller, some are shorter. It was very important, I thought, in the series to start having a variety of aliens so that they don't all look like Bossk in a different outfit. Is every Rodian from Rodia? It doesn't make any sense. Han Solo and Luke aren't from the same planet. Nor is Princess Leia. But they're all human beings. These aliens are spread out all over the galaxy—they're not just from one planet or place."

## MANY BOTHANS WERE CUT TO BRING US THIS EPISODE

Bothawui is the homeworld of the Bothans, first mentioned in *Return of the Jedi* as the spies who found the construction site of the second Death Star and revealed in Expanded Universe novels and comics as masters of bare-knuckles politics.

Bothans are masters at obtaining information—including some of the galaxy's deepest secrets. They're also very smart about making use of that information to benefit the Bothan species above all others. And, if need be, they'll sell information to the highest bidder. If other species don't like that, tough—Bothans know the way to survive in an often-hostile galaxy is by accumulating as much power and influence as possible. Henry Gilroy says he wanted to show the surface of Bothawui and see the plight of the planet's inhabitants preparing for war or readying to flee if there was a droid occupation.

### VEHICLE PROFILE

### *Vulture's Claw*

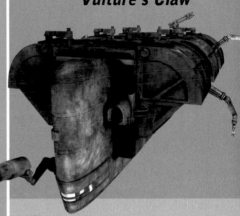

**Model:** GS-100 salvage ship

**Class:** Salvage ship

**Weapons:**
* Laser cannons

### EPISODE HIGHLIGHT

### IG-86 Assassin Droid

Among the deadliest droids in the galaxy, the IG-86 droids are more intelligent and skilled than the standard B1 battle droids.

## DROID PROFILE

### Astromech Droids

Astromech droids are all-around utility droids that serve as automated mechanics, performing a variety of repair duties. Because astromechs can perform more than 10,000 operations per second, many serve aboard specially designed starfighters and provide additional navigation and copilot duties.

## WEAPON PROFILE

### E-5 Droid Blaster

A powerful, lightweight blaster rifle that is standard issue for all battle droids.

## MANY BOTHANS WERE CUT TO BRING US THIS EPISODE (cont'd)

However, it was cut due to budget constraints." In choosing which parts of the Expanded Universe to explore, Gilroy says he uses galaxy maps passed on by Lucasfilm continuity editor Leland Chee.

"If we're using a specific species or culture, we would try to keep them consistent with their home worlds or their sector of the galaxy," he says. "Many references would be lost on the average *Clone Wars* viewer, so those are there for the serious fans who are well-versed in the Expanded Universe materials and would enjoy the references."

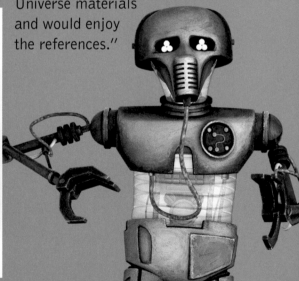

## Medical Droid

A type of droid found throughout the galaxy, they are roughly humanoid-appearing droids with surgical appendages, medical diagnostic computers, and treatment analysis computers.

# GALACTIC DISPATCHES
## THE SHADOW WAR

After R2-D2 sent R3-S6 on a one-way trip to the surface of Ruusan 2, Republic Intelligence discovered that Separatist slicers working at a forward supply base on Milagro had altered Goldie's programming. A number of astromechs on Milagro got replacement domes, letting the slicers introduce "sleeper" programs directing them to secretly contact Separatist forces in the vicinity and obey their orders. (The mismatch between Goldie's R3 designation and R2-class dome didn't arouse suspicions—astromechs were often repaired with non-standard parts.)

The Milagro Incident barely made news: Throughout the Clone Wars, Separatist and Republic spies sabotaged each other's factories, supply lines, and droids.

Separatist agents sabotaged the Druckenwell production line, which turned out tens of thousands of ammo cartridges that looked right but were too small to interlock with clone troopers' DC-15A rifles. At Handooine, they also introduced a virus into the computers of the *Tector*-class Gibbon, one of a handful of prototype Tectors and Imperators assigned to live-fire exercises as a prelude to formal production. The Gibbon virus replicated itself throughout Admiral Kreuge's task force, causing its capital ships to lower their shields once they approached a certain range at the Battle of Salvara. That turned a potentially pivotal Republic victory into a Separatist rout.

The Republic won victories, too: The Battle of Agomar was won when a Republic nano-virus caused destroyer droids and super battle droids to turn on each other, with legions of hapless B1 battle droids caught in the middle. And the Techno Union's leadership blamed Republic slicing for a host of behavioral anomalies seen in B1s that eroded the effectiveness of the Confederacy's droid armies.

## Episode 7:

I WILL DEAL WITH THE JEDI MYSELF.

# DUEL OF THE DROIDS

"You hold onto friends by keeping your heart a little softer than your head."

**Original Airdate:** 11/14/08

**Written by** Kevin Campbell, Henry Gilroy

**Directed by** Rob Coleman

**Cast**
Matt Lanter:
   Anakin Skywalker
Ashley Eckstein:
   Ahsoka Tano
Dee Bradley Baker:
   Clone troopers
Matthew Wood:
   General Grievous, battle
   droids
Ron Perlman:
   Gha Nachkt
James Arnold Taylor:
   Obi-Wan Kenobi
Tom Kane:
   Narrator

**Locations:** Skytop Station, Ruusan moon

## SYNOPSIS

Anakin tracks a distress call from a captured R2-D2 to a secret Separatist listening post, Skytop Station. Aboard the station, Anakin sends Ahsoka and Rex to destroy the ship's reactors while he searches for his droid. Grievous ambushes Ahsoka and Rex, but the young Padawan engages the General, while Rex continues with the mission. Meanwhile, Anakin rescues R2-D2. They make it to the ship's hangar, only to learn that R3-S6 is a Separatist spy. Rex detonates the explosions and Grievous flees the station. R2-D2 defeats R3-S6 in battle and is rescued from the exploding station at the last minute by Anakin.

KEEP MOVING, GREASE POT.

# NEWSREEL

Missing in action! Anakin Skywalker's heroic droid navigator R2-D2 was lost in battle. When a desperate search fails to locate R2, Anakin is forced to take on a new navigator, R3-S6. Now the Jedi embark on a dangerous new mission, to find a secret enemy listening post. Meanwhile, R2-D2 has fallen into the hands of a vile droid smuggler and is on his way to General Grievous, who will surely plunder the Republic's secrets hidden within him.... ∎

## ARTOO IS ARTOO

As with so many *Star Wars* stories, ultimately it's R2-D2 who saves the day, frees the *Twilight* from its hangar, and battles R3-S6 above a dizzying drop.

It's a fun action sequence, but not substantially different from anything you

**Vehicles:** Grievous's *Soulless One* (Belbullab-22 starfighter), *Twilight* (G9 Rigger), *Munificent*-class star frigate, Anakin Skywalker's Delta-7B *Aethersprite*-class starfighter, *Vulture's Claw* (Trandoshan scavenger ship), All Terrain Tactical Enforcer (AT-TE), *Acclamator I*-class assault ship, Battlesphere (*Lucrehulk*-class Core Ship), Porax-38 starfighter

**Weapons:** Lightsaber, restraining bolt, droid poppers (EMP grenade), DC-15A blaster rifle, DC-15S blaster, DC-17 blaster, E-5 blaster rifle, electrostaff

## CHARACTERS

Trooper Denal
General Grievous
Obi-Wan Kenobi
Gha Nachkt
R2-D2
R3-S6 ("Goldie")
Captain Rex
Anakin Skywalker
Ahsoka Tano

## TRIVIA

The seats in Gha Nachkt's *Vulture's Claw* are very similar to those aboard another beat-up freighter—the *Millennium Falcon*.

## Trooper Denal

A veteran clone trooper under Rex's command, Denal finds himself forced to improvise after R3-S6's repeated failures during the Skytop Station mission.

## EPISODE HIGHLIGHT

### ARTOO IS ARTOO (cont'd)

might see in a live action *Star Wars* story. Let's review: R2 saves Queen Amidala's Royal Starship in Episode I, rescues C-3PO from disassembly on Geonosis in Episode II, helps the *Millennium Falcon* escape Darth Vader in Episode V, and enables Luke Skywalker's rescue of Han Solo in Episode VI. And none of these rescues seems the least bit cartoony.

That's a fundamental rule for the series, says Henry Gilroy. "I never think of the show as animated—I think of the show as *Star Wars*," he says. "I would never write something for Artoo to do in the animated series that I wouldn't imagine him doing in live action. His duel with R3-S6 in this episode has some similarities with some of the action we saw from him in *Revenge of the Sith*."

## VEHICLE PROFILE

### P-38 Starfighter

**Model:** Porax-38 starfighter

**Class:** Starfighter

**Weapons:**
• Twin laser cannons

Gilroy notes that for all its thrills and chills, "Duel of the Droids" has a lot to say about the characters: "This was a great episode to showcase Anakin's affection and commitment to Artoo, even though he's not supposed to have attachments—especially such a strong one for a simple droid."

# Vulture Droid

These vicious mechanical killers are deadly on the ground and in space—they can walk on their wingtips and then spring into the air to engage Republic starfighters.

## WEAPON PROFILE
### Droid Popper

An electromagnetic pulse (EMP) grenade used to immobilize droids

## EPISODE HIGHLIGHT

## PADAWAN IN PERIL

One of the highlights of "Duel of the Droids" is seeing Ahsoka Tano lock lightsabers with the hulking General Grievous—though viewers may fear for Ahsoka's welfare, considering she's up against a deadly, tricky cyborg who's slain many Jedi and taken their lightsabers for trophies.

Considering the duel, Dave Filoni thought much the same thing. "At first glance, to myself even, I thought, 'Well, this is going to be a quick fight,'" he says. "Grievous is much larger than Ahsoka, and he's more powerful than Ahsoka. But as we often learn in *Star Wars*, size matters not." Which isn't to say Ahsoka can beat Grievous—despite her confidence, it's quickly obvious that she can't.

But the quick, catlike Togruta does okay.

"I think people have been surprised by how good Ahsoka is in some situations," Filoni says. "She can block bolts very well. She can fight quite well. In the movie we saw her standing up to the battle droids, but I would figure any Padawan who's well trained— particularly by Anakin Skywalker— would be able to hold their own. But when it came to fighting Ventress, in the brief encounter they had in the film, she got knocked over quite quickly. Ahsoka's no match for her—not yet. It's the same with Grievous."

Moreover, those who have seen *Revenge of the Sith* know Anakin can't rush to the rescue—aboard *Invisible Hand*, it's clear that the Chosen One and the

**PROFILE**

**Skytop Station**

**Model:** Battlesphere

**Class:** Space station

## R3-S6

Nicknamed "Goldie" by Ahsoka Tano, R3-S6 had his programming sabotaged by Separatist agents, and is secretly reporting to General Grievous.

## EPISODE HIGHLIGHT

GENERAL GRIEVOUS.

IT APPEARS THAT THIS MISSION MEMORY HAS NEVER BEEN ERASED.

IT CONTAINS EVERY REPUBLIC FORMATION AND STRATEGY THEY HAVE.

GOOD WORK. YOU HAVE CERTAINLY EARNED YOUR FEE THIS TIME.

MORE THAN MY FEE. THIS DROID IS WORTH MORE. I GET PAID MORE. NOW I SUGGEST . . .

HEH, HEH. THERE IS YOUR BONUS.

## PADAWAN IN PERIL (cont'd)

Separatist general are meeting for the first time, with Grievous sneering that he'd expected Anakin to be a little older and Anakin replying that the warlord is shorter than he'd expected.

An amusing moment, but one that tied Filoni's hands where *The Clone Wars* was concerned. "Here you have a situation where you have two major characters in *The Clone Wars* who can never really meet," he says. "They have fought each other fighter to fighter and ship to ship, but never face-to-face. It is a challenge, because I would like to see that fight."

Which of course leads to the kind of question about heroes and villains that's been debated in schoolyards for decades.

"I think Anakin, given Obi-Wan's performance in *Revenge of the Sith*, would take out Grievous fairly easily," Filoni says. "But you never know with Grievous. Grievous is deceitful. He's tricky. He will make the fight uneven and do whatever it takes to win."

## MagnaGuard

These Separatist droids were built as bodyguards for General Grievous, and mimic the look of Kaleesh warriors. Count Dooku has ordered more of them for his own use.

# GALACTIC DISPATCHES
## A FORGOTTEN WORLD

Skytop Station was hidden in the clouds of the Ruusan system, an anonymous moon of an obscure planet veiled by the dense nebulae of the thinly populated Teraab sector. From here, the Separatists could eavesdrop on Republic transmissions sent to points in the Mid Rim, Hutt Space, and parts of the Outer Rim—and there was little worry that a Republic battlegroup might stumble across them.

But nearly a thousand years before, Ruusan was the site of the final battle between Lord Hoth's Army of Light and Kaan's Brotherhood of Darkness. The Jedi and Sith armies clashed for two years, laying waste to Ruusan's green hills and terrorizing its human colonists and native "bouncers." The battle ended when Kaan detonated a Sith "thought bomb," imprisoning nearly all the Jedi and Sith spirits. That ended the war and—it seemed—destroyed the Sith as well. (Little did the Jedi know that the Sith renegade Darth Bane had escaped.)

Ruusan's Valley of the Jedi became a memorial to the Republic's victory and the Jedi's sacrifice. But within a couple of centuries, the ebb and flow of nebulae erased hyperspace routes leading to Ruusan, and the Jedi quietly had its location removed from star charts, hoping to keep away seekers of Sith knowledge.

The Valley of the Jedi became legend, and when the Hyper-Communications Cartel established Skytop Station, its leaders had no idea that the eyes of the galaxy had once been fixed on Ruusan—or that the spirits of thousands of Force-users remained entombed there.

# Episode 8:

THERE'S A BAD BOOGIE MONSTER DOWN DERE, YOU BETCHA.

# BOMBAD JEDI

"Heroes are made by the times."

## SYNOPSIS

Senator Padmé Amidala, Jar Jar Binks, and C-3PO head to the planet of Rodia to meet with Senator Onaconda Farr. However, they are tricked into a Separatist ambush and Padmé is taken prisoner. Jar Jar, wearing a Jedi robe that he found on the ship, heads out to rescue her. Nute Gunray and his droid army believe Jar Jar to be a real Jedi and unleash their full force to stop him. Luckily, a swamp monster, who Jar Jar met in the water below the city, arrives just in time to stop Gunray and the droids.

**Original Airdate:** 11/21/08

**Written by** Kevin Rubio, Henry Gilroy, Stephen Melching

**Directed by** Jesse Yeh

**Cast**
Anthony Daniels:
   C-3PO
Ahmed Best:
   Jar Jar Binks
Catherine Taber:
   Padmé Amidala
Matthew Wood:
   General Grievous, battle droids
Dee Bradley Baker:
   Onaconda Farr, clone troopers
Tom Kenny:
   Nute Gunray, Silood
Ian Abercrombie:
   Chancellor Palpatine
Tom Kane:
   Narrator

**Location:** Rodia

# NEWSREEL

The Clone War threatens the unity of the Republic! As battles rage across the galaxy, more worlds succumb to the seductive lure of the Separatists and leave the Republic. On a vital mission of peace, Senator Padmé Amidala journeys to the Outer Rim world of Rodia, desperate to ensure its loyalty remains to the Republic.... ∎

**Vehicles:** *Tranquility* (*Venator*-class Star Destroyer), Separatist boarding craft, *Munificent*-class star frigate, *Consular*-class space cruiser, Republic attack gunship, vulture droid starfighter

**Weapons:** lightsaber, DC-15A blaster rifle, DC-15s blaster, DC-17 hand blaster

## CHARACTERS

Senator Padmé Amidala
Jar Jar Binks
C-3PO
Onaconda Farr
Commander Gree
Nute Gunray
Silood

## EPISODE HIGHLIGHT

HANG ON, THREE-SO!

IT'S THREEPIO.

## A GUNGAN RECONSIDERED

"Bombad Jedi" marks *The Clone Wars* debut of Jar Jar Binks, who promptly gets in the kind of trouble Jar Jar Binks tends to get into.

Discussing the clumsy Gungan, Dave Filoni doesn't shy from admitting that some *Star Wars* fans—particularly older ones who grew up with the classic trilogy—may not have been thrilled to hear of Jar Jar's return. And he tries to get those fans to reconsider the Gungan.

"Jar Jar is a sad character in a lot of ways," Filoni says.

## Nute Gunray

The wicked Viceroy of the Trade Federation, Nute Gunray is a champion of the Separatist cause. He seeks revenge against Padmé Amidala for his defeat at Naboo.

## ALIEN PROFILE

### Gungans

Gungans breathe both air and water, and are comfortable on land—though much more graceful under the sea. After millennia of mutual suspicion, they now live in peace with the human colonists of Naboo.

## TRIVIA

The Kwazel Maw was originally conceived for *The Empire Strikes Back*, and imagined by Ralph McQuarrie as a predator in the lagoons of Dagobah.

## A GUNGAN RECONSIDERED (cont'd)

"He's the Fool. But he has very good intentions—he has a very good heart. We wanted to try and show that. He really cares about his friends, and he's trying to do well."

"Bombad Jedi" introduces a new pairing—Jar Jar and Threepio (whom Jar Jar keeps calling "Three-so"), who only had the briefest of interactions in Episode I. Putting them together turns out to have rich comedic potential, as well as a certain poignancy.

"Introducing Threepio alongside Jar Jar became very, very interesting, because we put one of the classic characters, who had some of the comedic moments in the original trilogy, with Jar Jar, who was the comedy in *The Phantom Menace*," Filoni says. "You had this old idea and this new idea, and Threepio at times is not very keen on Jar Jar."

C-3PO's disapproval, Filoni says, strikes

DON'T SHOOT.
WE SURRENDER.

a chord with "some of the older fans and how they feel about Jar Jar versus the newer fans and how they feel about Jar Jar. So maybe that parallel will help some people see some good in Jar Jar. Padmé obviously knows that Jar Jar is a hazard, but that doesn't mean she doesn't care about her friend and believe there's some value in him. Which is what Qui-Gon Jinn believed as well."

# Jar Jar Binks

A comically clumsy Gungan, Jar Jar Binks is seemingly always doing the wrong thing. Yet his friends also know that he's loyal, kindhearted, and means well.

## EPISODE HIGHLIGHT

## ALIEN PROFILE
### Rodians

A reptilian species, Rodians are loyal to their tight-knit clans. They are famous for their tracking skills, and some make their way in the galaxy as bounty hunters.

### A RODIAN FAIRY TALE

"Bombad Jedi" is a new story, but in classic *Star Wars* style it's one that follows a long-established template: that of the classic fairy tale.

"The fairy-tale archetypes are very literal in this story," Henry Gilroy says. "Padmé is the damsel in distress who is locked in the tower by the evil king, Nute Gunray. C-3PO is her faithful doting handmaiden. And Jar Jar is the court jester, who ends up in the armor of the knight: the Jedi robe of Anakin Skywalker. He's mistaken for the knight and struggles just to survive, but ends up saving the damsel and winning the day. My goal was always to help the audience relate to Jar Jar, in hopes it would spark some admiration for him."

### SENATOR IN A TIGHT SPOT

Central to the action of "Bombad Jedi" is Onaconda Farr, the Senator from Rodia and a lifelong friend of Padmé's. Farr's planet is caught between the armies of the Republic and the Separatists, his people are starving, and the Republic is stretched too thin to answer his pleas for help.

"He's desperate," Dave Filoni says. "So, like a desperate person, he makes a bad deal with Nute Gunray," who says that if Farr joins the Separatists and hands Padmé over to the Neimoidians, he'll give the people of Rodia the food and supplies they need.

"But Nute Gunray's a liar—that's not going to happen," Filoni says. "Onaconda Farr just doesn't know it yet. It's kind of like with Lando Calrissian—you know, 'This deal's getting worse all the time.' So I sold out my friend for you, where's the food? Wait, now you have my friend locked up in a tower? Why are all these battle droids here? Why are you occupying the city?"

Farr, like Lando in *The Empire Strikes Back*, soon realizes he's made a bad deal—and has to figure out a way out

## Onaconda Farr

This Senator from Rodia has known Padmé since she was a little girl. With his people starving, he makes a desperate bargain with the Separatists.

**EPISODE HIGHLIGHT**

## ALIEN PROFILE
### Kwazel Maw

A feared predator of Rodia's seas, the Kwazel Maw is nearly 100 meters. It generally lives in the depths, where it stuns prey with brilliant flashes of its bioluminescent markings.

## EPISODE HIGHLIGHT

POOR JAR JAR, HE WAS ALWAYS SUCH A MISFIT.

## SENATOR IN A TIGHT SPOT (cont'd)

of it. Which he does—but only with considerable help and forgiveness from Padmé, who lets him save face.

"In the end, Padmé believes in her friend Onaconda," Filoni says. "She believes that he's still a good person. She believes that he regrets the decision he's made. Onaconda didn't look at the real repercussions of the deal he made. So, as a good person, Padmé gives him an out in the end— she allows him to redeem himself and be a part of arresting Nute Gunray, rather than take Onaconda down for making that deal."

As Filoni sees it, on one level Padmé is just being a good politician, who knows that having Rodia as a Republic ally is more important than punishment for Farr. But, he adds, her decision also "shows you a little bit about Padmé's character and what she's made of that she can be so forgiving."

### Silood

Onaconda Farr's longtime attendant, Silood is a quiet presence at the Senator's side, offering whispered advice when he thinks it proper.

# GALACTIC DISPATCHES
## A LIFELONG BOND

As a young girl who dreamed of serving the galaxy, Padmé Naberrie followed the example of her father, Ruwee, who was tireless in his efforts on behalf of the Refugee Relief Movement (RRM).

The RRM's ideals held that the best thing a Republic citizen could do was to help beings on less-fortunate worlds. Furthermore, with millions upon millions of habitable worlds, any citizen of a Republic world should be allowed to find a new home when conditions threatened their own planet's well-being. Different branches of the movement tried to solve different problems plaguing galactic society, but the most celebrated branch of the RRM was the one dedicated to rescuing the people of worlds that had suffered natural disasters.

When Padmé was a child, Ruwee—then president of the RRM—addressed the Galactic Senate from Senator Palpatine's box, pleading for them to pass legislation to rescue millions from massive groundquakes on Sev Tok. Ruwee's eloquent speech moved many Senators, and Rodia's Onaconda Farr championed the cause and played a key role in pushing legislation through committees. Their efforts led to a lasting friendship, and several years later "Uncle Ono" served as the sponsor for Padmé when she decided to follow her father into the RRM service.

# Episode 9:

OPEN THIS DOOR AND I'LL BUY YOU A PLANET!

# CLOAK OF DARKNESS

"Ignore your instincts at your peril."

## SYNOPSIS

Jedi Ahsoka Tano and Luminara Unduli have been tasked with escorting Nute Gunray back to Coruscant. Clone Commander Gree and a team of Senate commandos, under the command of Captain Argyus, have been sent to guard Gunray. However, a team of super battle droids, led by Asajj Ventress, board their ship. As the two Jedi try to fight off the assassin, Captain Argyus reveals himself as a traitor and frees Gunray—however, his treachery is repaid by Ventress's lightsaber in his back.

**Original Airdate:** 12/5/08

**Written by** Paul Dini

**Directed by** Dave Filoni

**Cast**
Matt Lanter:
    Anakin Skywalker
Ashley Eckstein:
    Ahsoka Tano
Olivia d'Abo:
    Luminara Unduli
Tom Kenny:
    Nute Gunray
Nika Futterman:
    Asajj Ventress
James Marsters:
    Captain Argyus
Dee Bradley Baker:
    Clone troopers
Corey Burton:
    Count Dooku, Senate Guard
Ian Abercrombie:
    Darth Sidious
Tom Kane:
    Yoda, narrator

# NEWSREEL

Viceroy Gunray captured! Senator Padmé Amidala has scored a victory against the Separatist Alliance on the remote world of Rodia, securing the arrest of the diabolical Confederate leader, Nute Gunray. The Jedi Council has dispatched Master Luminara Unduli and Anakin Skywalker's Padawan, Ahsoka, to escort the Viceroy to Coruscant under heavy guard. Once there, he will face trial for his many war crimes.... ▇

**Location:** *Tranquility*

**Vehicles:** *Tranquility* (*Venator*-class Star Destroyer), Separatist boarding craft, *Munificent*-class star frigate, *Consular*-class space cruiser, Republic attack gunship, vulture droid starfighter

**Weapons:** lightsaber, DC-15A blaster rifle, DC-15S blaster, DC-17 hand blaster

## CHARACTERS

Captain Argyus
Count Dooku
Commander Gree
Nute Gunray
Darth Sidious
Anakin Skywalker
Ahsoka Tano
Luminara Unduli
Asajj Ventress
Yoda

## LADIES FIRST

"We had an interesting situation in 'Cloak of Darkness' where Ahsoka was assigned to be with Luminara," Dave Filoni says, explaining that when given a chance to finally bring Nute Gunray to justice, Anakin sent his own

## Commander Gree

Formally known as CC-1004, Gree is Luminara Unduli's second-in-command. A disciplined clone officer, he is baffled by the idea that a man like Argyus could betray the Republic that he serves.

## ALIEN PROFILE

### Neimoidians

As grubs, Neimoidians compete viciously for food, with the weak left to die. It's no wonder, then, that Neimoidians grow up to be intensely greedy beings who care little if others suffer.

## VEHICLE PROFILE

### Separatist Boarding Craft

**Model:** *Droch*-class boarding craft

**Class:** Boarding ship

**Weapons:**
* Crushing pincers

## LADIES FIRST (cont'd)

Padawan to help the more experienced Unduli guard him.

This says a lot about Anakin and Ahsoka—and soon reveals something about Ahsoka and Luminara.

"You get to see a little more clearly how Anakin's teaching style has affected Ahsoka," Filoni says. "Luminara wasn't expecting this young girl who's a bit brash. Ahsoka definitely says what she wants. This is different for Luminara—Luminara did not train Barriss Offee that way. So there's a contrast between the way Luminara sees Ahsoka and the way Anakin sees Ahsoka."

Now throw in another strong female character—the assassin Asajj Ventress.

TELL US WHAT WE WANT TO KNOW RIGHT NOW . . .

. . . OR I WILL GUT YOU LIKE A ROKARIAN DIRT-FISH!

"Ventress and Ahsoka, in the end, have a lot of things in common," Filoni says. "They're both students trying to impress their masters. Ventress just happens to be older than Ahsoka and further along in her training, so she's more powerful than Ahsoka. Ahsoka doesn't really stand a chance against Ventress—she can only hope to fight her off."

Strong female characters are a *Star Wars* staple, of course—we've

## Luminara Unduli

A by-the-book Jedi from the planet Mirial, Luminara Unduli believes that Padawans should follow their Masters' orders without question, and that discipline will always win out over passion and rage.

## EPISODE HIGHLIGHT

WHY'D YOU DO IT, ARGYUS?

A CLONE LIKE YOU WOULD NEVER UNDERSTAND. I WANTED A LIFE WITH MORE THAN EMPTY SERVITUDE.

AND, FOR THAT, YOU'D BETRAY THE REPUBLIC?

LIKE I TOLD THE PADAWAN: SOMETIMES BEING A GOOD SOLDIER MEANS DOING WHAT YOU THINK IS RIGHT.

YOU AND I DISAGREE ON WHAT MAKES A GOOD SOLDIER.

### LADIES FIRST (cont'd)

barely met Princess Leia Organa when we see her gun down a stormtrooper, and she proves an excellent shot with a blaster during combat in the bowels of the Death Star and the corridors of Cloud City. The same goes for her mother—Padmé may be a diplomat, but she's been known to reduce a battle droid or two to scrap during what she refers to as "aggressive negotiations." But the dynamic is different with a trio of lady Force-users.

Regarding the three female characters, Filoni says he likes "that they're all very different. Luminara's the conservative Jedi—she's old-school, more like Obi-Wan. Ahsoka's a hybrid, new-generation Jedi, being raised by Anakin Skywalker. And then, of course, there's the evil sister or the evil mother, who is Ventress. But even with Ventress, you find there's a lot of depth. She's trying so hard to please Dooku—she doesn't want to let him down. That's reflected by Ahsoka's attitude toward Anakin—in the end of the episode, she says 'I'm sorry I let you down, Master.' It's nice to have those parallels and then see how drastically different they are between good and evil."

## "TWO IN THE BACK"

The death of Captain Argyus comes as a shock, but Henry Gilroy says that as originally written, it was even more brutal: "Ventress ran him through with *both* sabers. When Dooku contacted her for an update and asked what happened to him, she smiled evilly and said, 'He took two in the back.'"

## PROFILE
### Senate Guards

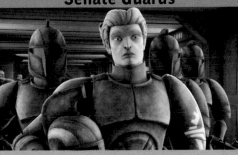

These blue-armored soldiers are one of Coruscant's proudest traditions, having protected the Senate for centuries. The best and bravest "Blue Guards" become commandos and are sent on secret Senate missions.

## EPISODE HIGHLIGHT

IF IT ISN'T THE HAIRLESS HARPY.

IF IT ISN'T SKYWALKER'S FILTHY, OBNOXIOUS LITTLE PET. STAND DOWN, LITTLE GIRL, AND I'LL GIVE YOU A COOKIE.

HOW NICE OF YOU. TELL YOU WHAT. I'LL GIVE YOU A MERCIFUL DEATH.

## Captain Argyus

A Senate commando from a proud Core World family, Argyus has lost faith in the Republic and in himself, agreeing to betray the cause his family has served for generations for Separatist credits.

## "TWO IN THE BACK" (cont'd)

If that's a bit of a shock, well, that's the point. "We never intend for the violence to be gratuitous, but to show that the villains won't hesitate to kill someone who is in their way creates a threat that is real to our heroes," Gilroy says. "Also, the show is about war and the nature of war is that characters will get killed and those deaths can be intense. Having a character we've come to know die creates suspense, because you never know who might die next."

## Darth Sidious

The secret leader of the Separatists, Darth Sidious is a shadowy Sith Lord who gives orders to Count Dooku. Sidious has a master plan for the Clone Wars which has yet to be revealed.

# GALACTIC DISPATCHES
## TRAITOR IN THE RANKS

Argyus's treachery shocked Republic loyalists: The Senate commandos were drawn from the best and bravest of the Senate Guards, the "Blue Wall" that had kept the galaxy's legislators safe from harm for generations. And Argyus was fifth-generation Blue Guard, from a Tepasi family famous for loyalty and honor.

But some saw Argyus's fall as just more proof that everything they held dear was crumbling. The Republic had turned itself into a military monster, sending an army of vat-grown clones to die against the Separatists. And while the Separatists' methods might be wrong, it was hard to argue with many of their complaints about the corrupt and bureaucratic Senate.

Even the Blue Guard wasn't what it had been. The crests of its azure helmets had been trimmed, and those who came face-to-face with Senate Guards now looked into blank black visors, unable to see the eyes of the men and women wearing the armor. And then there were the new Red Guards, created under mysterious circumstances for the sole purpose of guarding Chancellor Palpatine—the man who talked about how much he wanted to give up power even as he accumulated more and more of it.

In a galaxy like that, what was five generations of loyalty if it left you nothing but an anonymous servant of crooked politicians who had led the galaxy into war? Hadn't many on Coruscant thought of how nice it would be to have credits, freedom, and a place on some quiet world far from all this madness?

# Episode 10:

REVENGE IS NOT THE JEDI WAY.

# LAIR OF GRIEVOUS

"Most powerful is he who controls his own power."

**Original Airdate:** 12/12/08

**Written by** Henry Gilroy

**Directed by** Atsushi Takeuchi

**Cast**

Phil LaMarr:
   Kit Fisto
Matthew Wood:
   General Grievous, battle droids
Tom Kenny:
   Nahdar Vebb, Nute Gunray
Dee Bradley Baker:
   Clone troopers
David Acord:
   Droid A4-D
Corey Burton:
   Count Dooku
Tom Kane:
   Yoda, narrator
Ashley Eckstein:
   Ahsoka Tano
Terrence "TC" Carson:
   Mace Windu
Olivia d'Abo:
   Luminara Unduli

## SYNOPSIS

Kit Fisto tracks Gunray to the moon of Vassek. There, he is met by his former Padawan, Nahdar Vebb, and a team of clone troopers. Gunray's location is revealed to be in a strange stone fortress. However, once inside, they realize that they've been tricked by Count Dooku. Realizing that they're in General Grievous's lair, they plan a trap for him. But Grievous soon gets the upper hand and Nahdar finds himself alone and overpowered against Grievous. Trapped in Grievous's control room, Kit can only watch as his former Padawan is shot down.

**Location:** Vassek

**Vehicles:** Grievous's *Soulless One* (Belbullab-22 starfighter), Kit Fisto's Delta-7B *Aethersprite*-class starfighter, *Nu*-class attack shuttle

**Weapons:** DC-17 blaster, DC-15A blaster rifle, E-5 blaster rifle, rocket launcher, electrostaff, lightsaber

## NEWSREEL

Viceroy Gunray escapes! En route to Coruscant to stand trial for war crimes, evil Separatist leader Nute Gunray has broken free of his Jedi escort. With the help of Count Dooku's sinister agents, the villainous Viceroy has made a daring getaway. Alerted to the bold prison break, Jedi Master Kit Fisto has traced the stolen ship to a remote system, hoping to recapture Gunray and return him to justice.... ■

## THE CREEPY HOUSE ON VASSEK LANE

"Lair of Grievous" owes a debt to mysteries, horror matinees, and all other stories in which someone in the audience feels compelled to stand up and yell at the characters, "No! Don't go in the house!"

"The genesis of this episode was inspired by those old adventure serials where the hero goes into the dark creepy house of the villain and finds it full of deathtraps and monsters and terrible things and he has to fight tooth and nail just to get out," Henry Gilroy says, adding, "I have always been intrigued by the question, 'Where does evil live?'

## CHARACTERS

A4-D
Trooper Bel
Count Dooku
Commander Fil
Kit Fisto
General Grievous
Nute Gunray
Trooper Niner
R6-H5
Ahsoka Tano
Luminara Unduli
Nahdar Vebb
Mace Windu
Yoda

## Nahdar Vebb

A Mon Calamari Jedi who has just passed the trials and become a full Jedi Knight, Nahdar Vebb is impatient with the old Jedi traditions, which he thinks are of little use against the Separatist threat.

## THE CREEPY HOUSE ON VASSEK LANE (cont'd)

Grievous's lair really is a reflection of him as a character—it's cold and hard on the outside and completely rotten on the inside."

## THE ONE WITH ALL THE FISH

Discussing "Lair of Grievous," Dave Filoni notes that the episode has almost no human faces—other than brief appearances (via holograph) by Count Dooku and Mace Windu, the only faces we see belong to aliens, droids, and mixtures of the two. Moreover, the two main heroes are the Nautolan Jedi Kit Fisto and the Mon Calamari Jedi Nahdar Vebb, leaving Filoni to call this installment of *The Clone Wars* "the all-fish episode."

Filoni's joking, but the lack of human faces does present a potential difficulty in connecting with the audience.

"We had a little Calamari guy hanging out with a Nautolan, which is basically looking

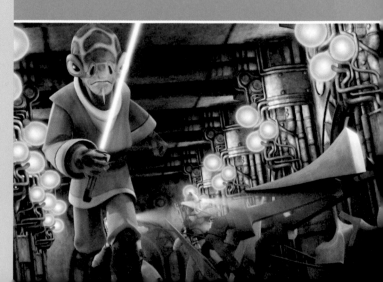

SOMETIMES I WONDER WHY YOU SUBMITTED TO THE CHANGES.

IMPROVEMENTS! I SUBMIT TO NO ONE—I CHOSE THEM! NOW GET ON WITH IT.

at two sushi pieces walk around," Filoni says. "The challenge became, 'How about their characters?' They have to be interesting."

Fortunately, in Fisto and Nahdar, Filoni has two interesting characters. Fisto has been a fan favorite since Episode II, when he flashed a sly smile even as the Battle of Geonosis raged around him. His patience and charm (brought nicely to life by Phil LaMarr) is set against the impatience and anger of his former Padawan.

Nahdar has recently taken the trials and been granted the status of Jedi Knight, but the viewer soon suspects he's not ready to be a Jedi.

"Nahdar is a representation of where some of the younger Jedi are going," Filoni says. "They get a bit confused in the war. They think

## Kit Fisto

A Nautolan Jedi, Kit Fisto has a gentle manner and a quick laugh. But he's also one of the Jedi Order's fiercest fighters, as many an enemy of the Republic has discovered.

## ALIEN PROFILE

### Mon Calamari

The Mon Calamari hail from a planet near the edge of the galaxy, and are famous for their gifts as starship designers and builders. Their homeworld has suffered terribly from Separatist attacks.

## EPISODE HIGHLIGHT

HOW QUICKLY POWER CAN CHANGE HANDS.

SURRENDER, AND I PROMISE YOU WILL DIE QUICKLY.

## THE ONE WITH ALL THE FISH (cont'd)

the war has changed things—that now they need to use more power, that they shouldn't follow the old teachings that they were taught as younglings, that they should seize power and use that to overcome their enemies. Kit Fisto says, 'Power will only consume you'—he even warns Grievous about that."

As Filoni notes, "Grievous is another person who has tried to seize greater power in order to gain something in his life that he couldn't get through peaceful means. So there's a parallel between Nahdar and Grievous. Now, at the end of the day, Grievous is a cheater. He will block your lightsaber, pull a gun out and shoot you—which, unfortunately for Nahdar, is what happens. So Nahdar's quest for power ends abruptly when he becomes shortsighted and doesn't realize that his enemy—Grievous—is much more diabolical and much more dangerous than he first thought. Nahdar overestimates his own power, much to Kit Fisto's dismay."

By the time that drama has played out, Filoni

says, "we've forgotten that they're just two fish guys running around. In the end, I think, the characters rise above their masks. You see through the big tentacle head of Kit Fisto to the character he is, and you see Nahdar for the character he is. And you let go of the fact that, you know, one of them looks like a goldfish."

## THE JEDI'S SMILE

Dave Filoni says that "Kit Fisto's development was pretty easy, actually"—it started with that smile in *Attack of the Clones*.

"It's a very bizarre moment in this big battle, but it's why people latched on to Kit Fisto and said, 'Wow, I really like this guy,'" he says. "It gave him some character—he wasn't just this stuffy Jedi meditating in the Temple all the time."

But what voice should go with that smile?

"George felt very strongly that he should have a Jamaican accent—I guess because everybody jokes that his head-tails are like dreadlocks anyway," Filoni says. "We just tried to do it subtly so it didn't really jump out at you too much.

YOU EXPECT VICTORY OVER THE JEDI, BUT ALL YOU GIVE ME TO FIGHT THEM ARE BATTLE DROIDS! BAH!

WHAT ABOUT YOUR FORMER PADAWAN?

HIS HEART WAS IN THE RIGHT PLACE, BUT HE TRIED TO ANSWER GRIEVOUS'S POWER WITH HIS OWN.

TO ANSWER POWER WITH POWER, THE JEDI WAY THIS IS NOT. IN THIS WAR, A DANGER THERE IS OF LOSING WHO WE ARE.

## A4-D

The surgical droid A4-D is responsible for keeping General Grievous in good health and good repair, and also serves as caretaker for the General's redoubt on Vassek.

## ALIEN PROFILE

### Roggwarts

**Homeworld:** Guiteica

Years before the Clone Wars, an army of Kaleesh and Jedi stormed the planet Guiteica, home to the Bitthævrian warriors. Many Kaleesh, including Grievous, took home baby roggwarts, training the creatures to be devoted pets and fierce watch-beasts.

## THE JEDI'S SMILE (cont'd)

It gave him a little bit more character and a little bit more interest."

Filoni sees Fisto as outwardly more positive than other Jedi Masters, such as the wise but solemn Plo Koon. But at the same time, the Nautolan Jedi is philosophical and able to let go. In "Lair of Grievous," Fisto lets go of his former Padawan, whom he can't save from an obsession with power, and he lets go of his pride, retreating rather than trying to fight both Grievous and his bodyguards.

"He definitely has a lot of compassion—he definitely wants to try and save Nahdar," Filoni says of Kit Fisto. "But unlike Anakin, at the end he knows Nahdar made a mistake. He lets go of Nahdar because that was Nahdar's fate. It's an important episode about attachments, without talking specifically about attachments. Anakin would never have let go so easily, were that to have happened to Ahsoka."

## R6-H5

R6-H5 is Kit Fisto's astromech, and accompanies him to remote Vassek. Something of a worrywart, R6 is one of a number of Republic astromechs used for testing new prototype droid systems.

# GALACTIC DISPATCHES
## GOR THE ROGGWART

Roggwarts are native to Guiteica, a neighbor of Grievous's homeworld of Kalee. Guiteica was home to the Bitthævrians, a species of proud warriors who wanted little to do with the Republic or its corrupt politics.

Years before the Clone Wars, the Republic worried that the Bitthævrians could be a threat to the galaxy, and an army of Jedi and Kaleesh stormed Guiteica and defeated their armies.

While the Kaleesh would eventually come to hate the Republic, at the time they celebrated the Bitthævrian War as having shown the galaxy their might in battle. The Kaleesh also respected their Bitthævrian opponents, who had fought fiercely but honorably. Many took trophies from Guiteica—and the most valuable trophies were the creatures known as roggwarts.

Xenobiologists argued over whether roggwarts were an offshoot of the Bitthævrian species, had been created from them through genetic tinkering, or simply looked similar through convergent evolution. Whatever the case, they were ferocious predators, with razor-sharp claws and strong jaws. If taken from their brood-nests early enough, they could be trained as watch-guardians or pets, and proved obedient and even devoted.

After the Bitthævrian War, no respectable Kaleesh warlord was without a roggwart or two. General Grievous named his Gor, and doted on the fearsome creature, housing it in his lair on Vassek. To Grievous, Kit Fisto murdering Gor was just one more wrong for which the Jedi Order would pay dearly.

# Episode 11:

YOU DON'T SURVIVE IN THE OUTER RIM BY BEING STUPID!

# DOOKU CAPTURED

"The winding path to peace is always a worthy one, regardless of how many turns it takes."

**Original Airdate:** 1/2/09

**Written by** Julie Siege

**Directed by** Jesse Yeh

**Cast**
Matt Lanter:
   Anakin Skywalker
James Arnold Taylor:
   Obi-Wan Kenobi
Jim Cummings:
   Hondo Ohnaka
Corey Burton:
   Count Dooku
Ashley Eckstein:
   Ahsoka Tano
Ian Abercrombie:
   Chancellor Palpatine
Tom Kane:
   Yoda, narrator
Terrence "TC" Carson:
   Mace Windu
Greg Ellis:
   Turk
Dee Bradley Baker:
   Pilf Mukmuk

**Locations:** Coruscant, Vanqor, Florrum

## SYNOPSIS

Fleeing from an attempted ambush by Anakin Skywalker and Obi-Wan Kenobi, Count Dooku's ship crashes on the planet of Vanqor. Shortly after, Anakin and Obi-Wan's ship crashes in the same location. The two Jedi head into a cave to find Dooku, but he traps them in with an avalanche. He heads back to his ship to find it surrounded by pirates. Knowing that he's trapped, Dooku accepts their offer to fly him to a nearby planet. However, he arrives to find himself overpowered. The pirates wish to ransom him to the Republic, so Palpatine sends Anakin and Obi-Wan to confirm that they have Dooku. The two Jedi, however, find themselves captured by the pirates as well.

## NEWSREEL

Manhunt! After a long and perilous search, the Jedi finally track down Separatist leader Count Dooku. During a heroic attempt to capture the Count, Anakin Skywalker has gone missing. Having lost contact with Skywalker, Obi-Wan Kenobi heads toward his friend's last known location, a lone Separatist frigate in the far reaches of the Outer Rim.... ∎

**Vehicles:** *Munificent*-class star frigate, *Nu*-class attack shuttle, *Punworcca*-class interstelar sloop, *Sheathipede*-class transport shuttle, *Twilight* (G9 Rigger), Weequay pirate ship, Weequay saucer craft, *Sheathipede*-class transport shuttle, *Resolute* (*Venator*-class Star Destroyer)

**Weapons:** DC-15A blaster rifle, lightsaber, E-5 blaster rifle, Weequay rifle, DC-15S blaster

## THE FLYING SAUCER

Dave Filoni calls the saucer-shaped pirate ship in this episode "for all intents and purposes, a retro UFO. This is something that I think George has been trying to get into *Star Wars* for a very long time." (Filoni notes that a similar design is seen in production sketches of Alderaan for *Revenge of the Sith*.)

The ship will also summon memories of

## CHARACTERS

Senator Padmé Amidala
Jar Jar Binks
Count Dooku
Turk Falso
Obi-Wan Kenobi
Senator Kharrus
Plo Koon
Pilf Mukmuk
Hondo Ohnaka
Chancellor Palpatine
Captain Rex
Anakin Skywalker
Ahsoka Tano
Mace Windu
Yoda

## Count Dooku

The public leader of the Separatists, Count Dooku left the Jedi Order, dismayed at the corruption of the Republic, and now serves the Separatists' master.

## ALIEN PROFILE
### Weequays

Weequays are leathery-skinned bipeds native to the desert planet Sriluur, near the central worlds controlled by the Hutts. They frequently hire on with Hutt crime lords as bodyguards or mercenaries, though they are not one of the giant slugs' slave species.

## PLANET PROFILE
### Vanqor

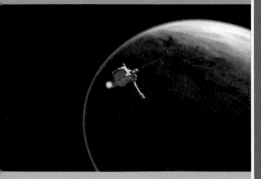

**Region:** Outer Rim

**Inhabitants:** Humans, gundarks

A desolate world far from the galaxy's population centers, Vanqor is known for its tough human inhabitants, as well as for the unfortunate number of gundark nests that dot its canyons, mountains, and badlands.

## THE FLYING SAUCER (cont'd)

old space-opera serials such as *Flash Gordon* and *Buck Rogers*—down to the retro sound of the spinning ship powering up.

The design for the main pirate ships came from Russell Chong, who Filoni calls his "resident UFO expert," and was originally copper and much dirtier and dingier-looking. But Lucas wanted it silver, again emphasizing the retro design. As for the little saucer-shaped pirate craft, Filoni says it was inspired by a Doug Chiang design for *The Phantom Menace*—another example of Lucas finding a home for a visual element he liked but had to discard.

"That he didn't get to use them in a feature doesn't mean he won't use them here," Filoni says of Lucas and such designs. "He has them in mind and he brings them up and next thing you know they're flying around *The Clone Wars*."

## A BIGGER GALAXY

The Weequay pirate Hondo Ohnaka nearly steals "Dooku Captured" from the main characters, grabbing the viewer's attention with his flamboyant personality and his cynical, knowing dialogue. His new fans should rejoice—Dave Filoni says the character will show up from time to time in the future.

"He's a new character for us in *The Clone Wars*, and arguably the characters that are very new are interesting immediately because you don't know what happens to them," he says, adding, "We always have to wonder,

## EPISODE HIGHLIGHT

HOW COME I'M THE ONE GETTING CAUGHT ALL THE TIME?

IT DOESN'T LOOK GOOD.

WHEN YOU'RE A JEDI MASTER, YOU CAN MAKE THE PLAN.

THAT'S JUST IT. HOW CAN I BECOME A JEDI MASTER IF I'M ALWAYS GETTING CAUGHT?

AT LEAST YOU'RE A MASTER AT GETTING CAUGHT.

## Hondo Ohnaka

A Weequay pirate, Hondo Ohnaka and his gang prowl the galaxy's remote spacelanes, kidnapping travelers and holding them for ransom.

## VEHICLE PROFILE

### Neimoidian Shuttle

**Model:** Sheathipede transport shuttle

**Class:** Shuttle

**Weapons:**
• Laser cannons

## EPISODE HIGHLIGHT

I AM MORE POWERFUL THAN ANY JEDI.

KNOW THAT YOU ARE DEALING WITH A SITH LORD.

YOU'RE STILL OUTNUMBERED.

## A BIGGER GALAXY (cont'd)

whose side is he playing? He's not with the Republic, he's not with the Separatists—he's an independent. He's not necessarily for hire, but he—like so many others—is trying to figure out how he can profit from the Clone Wars and what his role's going to be in the Clone Wars. It's interesting to see a character like that develop."

Moreover, Filoni says, characters like Hondo expand the narrative "beyond just, 'Oh the Jedi and the Republic are fighting the Sith and the Separatists.' It's a bigger galaxy than that, especially to George."

Yes, *Star Wars* is a tale of war and adventure on a galactic scale—it always has been and hopefully always will be. But not everybody in the saga is a Jedi Knight chosen by ancient prophecy to restore balance to the Force. There are characters with smaller-scale dramas, such as Hondo Ohnaka—simple souls trying to make their way in the universe, to quote a certain Mandalorian bounty hunter.

I STILL DON'T GET IT.

GET WHAT?

HOW A BUNCH OF PIRATES MANAGED TO CATCH DOOKU WHEN WE COULDN'T.

Filoni notes that Lucas "has tons of these characters that we didn't know about. George created Hondo—these stories come straight from George. These are things he wants to see in *The Clone Wars*, these are stories he wants to tell. And in the series we are developing these ideas and going further with them then he ever could [in the feature films]."

MAYBE THERE'S A LESSON TO BE LEARNED HERE.

In the movies, Filoni says, "Hondo would have been a background

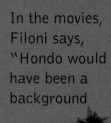

I STILL DON'T GET IT.

IT'S TO REMIND US TO BE HUMBLE . . .

## Pilf Mukmuk

A mischievous Kowakian monkey-lizard, Pilf Mukmuk is smarter than most people give him credit for, and helps capture Anakin and Obi-Wan.

AND NEVER TOO PROUD TO ACCEPT A GIFT WHEN IT COMES OUR WAY.

## ALIEN PROFILE

### Gundarks

Gundarks come in a variety of shapes and sizes and are found on different worlds, with some of the largest living on the desolate world of Vanqor. They are born with two arms and small ears, but later sprout additional arms and their ears grow dramatically.

## VEHICLE PROFILE

### Solar Sailer

**Model:** Sloop

**Class:** Punworcca 116 Interstellar Sloop

**Weapons:**
- Tractor/repulsor beam array

## A BIGGER GALAXY (cont'd)

character. Licensing would have figured out his name is Hondo and he would have shown up in some fourth or fifth wave of action figures. But here he is a speaking, living, breathing character that the main characters interact with—because we have time to tell these particular stories."

## Space Suits

Space suits are used by individuals to enter space, often for the purpose of doing repairs on the surface or in the depressurized compartments of starships or space stations. However, during the Clone Wars, space suits are often used by the military.

# GALACTIC DISPATCHES
## HONDO OHNAKA'S BIG SCORE

Hondo Ohnaka was born on Sriluur to small-time grifters who sold him into the service of the Great God Quay, revered as the bringer of Weequay luck both good and bad.

There are worse fates than being a child-servant of Quay, but Hondo thought believing that the whim of some divine being determined your entire life was crazy. As he saw it, he was a servant because his parents had been too poor to give him something better, and they had been poor because their parents had been poor—Quay didn't have anything to do with it.

Hondo stowed away on a ship to Boonta, where he became the cupbearer for Porla the Hutt. He eventually got up the courage to suggest his Master was being cheated: His smugglers claimed oddly high fees for spice-processing and cargo-loading, and only got pinched by Republic warships while carrying valuable cargos. After Hondo turned out to be right, he was always at Porla's side, listening to his business dealings and whispering in his ear.

Hondo and several other servants eventually ran off and set up on remote Florrum, raiding ships traveling between the Tion Hegemony and the Corporate Sector for hostages and parts. Florrum was a fine base for that, but not for bigger things. Hondo knew spice smuggling, and knew he could make far more credits than the Outer Rim's dumb, vicious criminals. But he needed an in—a stake big enough that he could parcel out the spice slowly and look like a player. Four hundred thousand credits' worth ought to do it. But that much spice wasn't just going to fall into his lap, now was it? You'd have to believe in Quay to be that much of an optimist.

# Episode 12:

ER . . . UH . . . WHAT? BOMBAD CLANKERS?

# THE GUNGAN GENERAL

"Fail with honor rather than succeed by fraud."

**Original Airdate:** 1/9/09

**Written by** Julie Siege

**Directed by** Justin Ridge

**Cast**
BJ Hughes:
    Jar Jar Binks
Matt Lanter:
    Anakin Skywalker
James Arnold Taylor:
    Obi-Wan Kenobi, Weequay
    henchman
Dee Bradley Baker:
    Clone troopers, pirate
    guard #2
Jim Cummings:
    Hondo Ohnaka
Corey Burton:
    Count Dooku, Senator
    Kharrus, pirate guard #1
Greg Ellis:
    Turk Falso
Ian Abercrombie:
    Chancellor Palpatine
Catherine Taber:
    Padmé Amidala

## SYNOPSIS

After being drugged by Weequay pirates, Anakin and Obi-Wan wake to find themselves in a prison cell and tethered to Count Dooku. Meanwhile, the clones arrive with Dooku's ransom. Their shuttle is shot down by Hondo's rival Turk Falso, and Senator Kharrus is killed, leaving Jar Jar in charge. After several failed escape attempts, the Jedi are finally freed when Jar Jar accidentally knocks out the pirates' power supply. In the confusion, Dooku escapes.

## NEWSREEL

Dooku held for ransom! After escaping capture by Jedi Knights Anakin Skywalker and Obi-Wan Kenobi, the villainous Count Dooku fell into the clutches of pirates led by the brigand Hondo Ohnaka. Eager to get custody of Dooku, the Republic agreed to pay Hondo a hefty sum in exchange for the Sith Lord. But Anakin and Obi-Wan had not counted on the treacherous cunning of Ohnaka and his band.... ∎

## LIGHT DURING WARTIME

Considering Obi-Wan, Anakin, and Dooku spend much of the episode at odds in close quarters, "The Gungan General" may strike fans as unexpectedly funny—the Jedi and the Sith squabble constantly, and their attempted escapes could have been borrowed from the Three Stooges.

Does that seems out of place during a galactic war? Not at all—to Henry Gilroy, it's pure *Star Wars* from George Lucas himself, who wanted to explore the absurdity of the Jedi and the Sith trapped in a bad

**Cast (continued)**
Tom Kane:
  Narrator
David Acord:
  Kowakian Monkey

**Locations:** Coruscant; Florrum

**Vehicles:** *Nu*-class attack shuttle, Weequay saucer craft, *Twilight* (G9 Rigger), pirate tank, pirate speeder bike

**Weapons:** DC-17 hand blaster, lightsaber, E-5 blaster rifle, Weequay rifle, DC-15S blaster

## CHARACTERS

4A-2R
Senator Padmé Amidala
Jar Jar Binks
Count Dooku
Turk Falso
Obi-Wan Kenobi
Senator Kharrus
Plo Koon
Pilf Mukmuk
Hondo Ohnaka
Chancellor Palpatine
Anakin Skywalker
Commander Stone
Mace Windu
R5-P8
Yoda

# Senator Kharrus

A three-eyed Gran, Kharrus is a veteran Senator used to the dangers of negotiations with the galaxy's more dangerous elements.

## DROID PROFILE
### Pirate Guards

Normally, droids like this R5 unit are programmed never to harm living beings. But Hondo Ohnaka's pirates have hacked the logic modules of captured astromechs, turning them into armed sentries (with painted-on smiles).

## ALIEN PROFILE
### Skalders

Barrel-chested grazers, skalders live on the plains of Florrum. They got their name from their habit of eating grass in the shadow of Florrum's geysers. But skalders can sense when a spume of superheated water is on the way, and their thick hides and great speed allow them to escape serious burns.

## LIGHT DURING WARTIME (cont'd)

situation together. The contrast between the serious and light-hearted is part of the *Star Wars* tradition, Gilroy notes—for example, "in one scene you watch a planet populated by billions destroyed by the Death Star, and in another you have Chewbacca frighten away a mouse droid with a growl."

"When we developed the stories for Season One," Gilroy says, "George directed us to have a variety of genres. Sure, there would be war dramas—but he wanted mystery, adventure, comedy, and romance, all of which can be found sprinkled throughout the films."

## PUTTING IT ALL TOGETHER

Dave Filoni describes "The Gungan General" as a difficult story to tell in part because it has so many elements—Dooku, Obi-Wan, and

YOU WANT TO DEACTIVATE THE CELL BARS.

I . . . I . . . WANT TO . . .

YOU WANT TO DEACTIVATE THE CELL BARS AND GO OUT DRINKING.

I WANT TO DEACTIVATE THE CELL BARS AND GO OUT DRINKING!

Anakin have to try to escape together, exchanging jibes the whole time, and on top of that, Jar Jar Binks is the one trying to rescue them.

"George sometimes will do that—he'll challenge us," Filoni says.

"He'll say, 'Well, I want Count Dooku to get captured by pirates and then Anakin and Obi-Wan will get captured along with him and the three of them have to break out of jail together and I want Jar

# Commander Stone

Formally known as CC-5869, Stone is a commander with the Coruscant Guard's Diplomatic Escort Group.

## PLANET PROFILE

### Florrum

**Region:** Outer Rim

**Inhabitants:** Skalders

A bleak planet located near Vanqor, Florrum isn't exactly a garden spot even by the low standards of the Outer Rim. But its proximity to a lawless trading route makes it the perfect location for a pirate lair.

## VEHICLE PROFILE

### Pirate Speeder Bike

**Model:** Starhawk speeder bike

**Class:** Speeder bike

**Weapons:**
• None

## PUTTING IT ALL TOGETHER (cont'd)

Jar to come and try and rescue them.' Amazing, you know? Wow, how are we going to do that?"

An early concept of the story, Filoni says, was focused on Jar Jar and the clones: The clones' officer died in a shuttle crash, and Jar Jar was left in charge as the ranking official.

"It was up to Jar Jar to get them from Point A to Point B past a barricade of Separatist tanks," Filoni says. "It was really just a squad of soldiers vs. tanks, led by Jar Jar. That

### Shuttle Pilot
Clones who have shown to have exceptional reflexes are trained by the Kaminoans to pilot a variety of Republic craft, from warships to shuttles and gunships.

JEDI! AFTER EVERYTHING, YOU'RE JUST GOING TO WALK AWAY?

WE HAVE NO QUARREL WITH YOU AND WE SEEK NO REVENGE.

was the initial idea, and then the whole pirate plot got put on top of it—Dooku got captured in the previous episode and this became a sequel. That's sometimes how these stories are developed—they change, and suddenly they're about a whole lot more."

INDEED. VERY HONORABLE, MASTER JEDI.

## OBI-WAN'S FORGIVENESS

With Dooku escaped and Obi-Wan and Anakin free, Hondo Ohnaka expects a fight—but Kenobi is willing to walk away. The pirate is surprised—and so, perhaps, is the audience.

OH, CAPTAIN, YOU WILL FIND THAT COUNT DOOKU DOES NOT SHARE OUR SENSE OF HONOR . . . AND HE KNOWS WHERE YOU LIVE.

YOU SHOULD BE MORE PATIENT, MASTER. AFTER ALL, THE COUNT IS AN ELDERLY GENTLEMAN AND DOESN'T MOVE LIKE HE USED TO.

I SUPPOSE YOU'RE RIGHT.

## VEHICLE PROFILE

### Pirate Tank

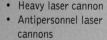

**Model:** Ubrikkian Ord Pedrovia WLO-5 speeder tank

**Class:** Speeder

**Weapons:**
- Heavy laser cannon
- Antipersonnel laser cannons

## OBI-WAN'S FORGIVENESS (cont'd)

"Hondo has done all these terrible things to Obi-Wan—he imprisoned Obi-Wan and Anakin, he deceived Obi-Wan and Anakin, Hondo's responsible for letting a terrible evil loose back into the galaxy after they had him penned up," Dave Filoni says. "Despite all those things, Obi-Wan's forgiving. He says, 'Let him go, Anakin' and they're going to walk away. Because for Obi-Wan there is no conflict anymore. 'You don't have anything I want, I'm not a hostage anymore, so we're done.' And Hondo has a hard time understanding that Obi-Wan would just walk away. In Hondo's world, it's an eye for an eye—it's cause and effect."

By confounding Hondo's expectations, Filoni says, Obi-Wan "proves his worth as a hero—he has no grievance with Hondo anymore. But Dooku will not forget this. And that gives Hondo cause to think about what he's really done."

## Turk Falso

Hondo's lieutenant, the Weequay Turk Falso, decides to betray his boss in hopes of taking over the leadership of the Ohnaka Gang.

# GALACTIC DISPATCHES
## HELP WHERE YOU LEAST EXPECT IT

When Hondo Ohnaka's gang set up shop on Florrum, they found its plains dotted with geysers—good as a source of geothermal power for a base, but not so good if you dislike the possibility of being boiled alive by an eruption of superheated steam. And Florrum had a truly depressing lack of things pirates liked to eat: There was nary a nerf, fleek eel, or roba to be seen. The dominant grazing animals of the fields were plodding beasts the pirates called skalders, amused by the grazers' dimwitted habit of munching grasses in the very shadow of the geysers' mouths. After arriving on Florrum, the gang promptly shot several skalders, but the meat smelled terrible while it was being prepared and tasted worse. It didn't matter whether you boiled it, broiled it, poached it, seared it, or even fricasseed it—skalder was absolutely vile to eat.

The pirates soon forgot all about the skalders, except when things got so boring that it seemed like a good idea to jump on speeder bikes and shoot a couple for sport. Had Hondo's gang bothered to learn the slightest bit about their habits, they might have noticed something that didn't escape the eye of even a flighty Gungan: Skalders can detect when geysers are about to burst, enabling them to run through geyser fields without being caught in an eruption.

## Episode 13:

HURRY, SKYWALKER, WE ARE DEPENDING ON YOU.

# JEDI CRASH

"Greed and fear of loss are the roots that lead to the tree of evil."

**Original Airdate:** 1/16/09

**Written by** Katie Lucas

**Directed by** Rob Coleman

**Cast**
Ashley Eckstein:
    Ahsoka Tano
Jennifer Hale:
    Aayla Secura
Matt Lanter:
    Anakin Skywalker
Dee Bradley Baker:
    Clone troopers
Tom Kane: Admiral Yularen,
    narrator
George Coe:
    Tee Watt Kaa
Alec Medlock:
    Wag Too
Matthew Wood:
    Battle droids, tactical droid

## SYNOPSIS

Anakin is severely injured rescuing Aayla Secura from an attack on her Star Destroyer. During their escape, their frigate is damaged and crashes on the remote world of Maridun. Ahoska is worried about her Master and seeks help from the local Lurmen, who are peaceful and reject the Jedi and clones. Their leader, Tee Watt Kaa, eventually allows his son, Wag Too, who is a healer, to help Anakin.

## NEWSREEL

The Republic fleet is on the defensive and pushed to the brink! As war rages in the much contested Outer Rim Territories, chaos and fear mount as the Separatist army wages an epic battle against heavily outnumbered Republic ships in the far reaches of the Quell system. Anakin Skywalker and his Padawan Ahsoka race across the galaxy to aid Jedi Knight Aayla Secura, who is in the midst of a fight for her life as the sinister droid army closes in.... ∎

**Locations:** Quell, Maridun

**Vehicles:** *Venator*-class Star Destroyer, Republic frigate, *Munificent*-class star frigate, V-19 Torrent starfighter, Republic attack gunship

**Weapons:** DC-15S blaster, E-5 blaster, DC-17 hand blaster, lightsaber, E-5 blaster rifle

## ENTER THE LURMEN

Henry Gilroy says in the first season of *The Clone Wars*, he often worked on the characterizations and plot for a story while Dave Filoni was developing visual concepts: "I might pitch him an idea about a story on a particular planet, and he would come up with ideas about what the planet looks like and what sort of creatures and aliens might live there."

## CHARACTERS

Commander Bly
Trooper Cameron
Trooper Flash
Tee Watt Kaa
Trooper Lucky
Captain Rex
Aayla Secura
Anakin Skywalker
Tactical Droid
Ahsoka Tano
Wag Too
Tub
Admiral Wullf Yularen

## EPISODE HIGHLIGHT

# Commander Bly

Bly, formally known as CC-5052, serves Aayla Secura and is intensely loyal to her, though suspicious of how reckless other Jedi generals can be.

WELL, WE'RE NOT GOING TO CRASH INTO THE STAR, BUT WE'RE DEFINITELY GOING TO HIT THAT PLANET.

## EPISODE HIGHLIGHT

ARE ALL JEDI SO RECKLESS?

JUST THE GOOD ONES.

## ALIEN PROFILE
### Lurmen

The Lurmen are native to Mygeeto, a planet controlled by the Separatist Banking Clan. They are both speedy and smart, combining lightning-quick reflexes with superb eyesight, hearing, and a sense of smell. Those keen senses are needed to survive on a world as hostile as Maridun.

## ENTER THE LURMEN (cont'd)

In the case of "Jedi Crash," there was a change of plans. Originally, the stranded Jedi and clones encountered the Amanin, green reptilian aliens first glimpsed in Jabba's palace during *Return of the Jedi*. The Amanin were brought to life in a notable series by Dark Horse Comics, which portrayed them fighting ceaselessly against a group of Imperial soldiers to uphold their sense of honor. Those Amanin were terrible opponents, ones who would have given "Jedi Crash" a rather different feel, to say the least.

But as Gilroy recalls, "When George read the script, he wanted the aliens to be a little warmer and more expressive as mammals, and gave us an unused design from *Revenge of the Sith*."

That design was the Lurmen, who pushed the Amanin out of the picture. But fans who know their Expanded Universe lore will find nods to the original species: "Jedi Crash" takes place on the Amanin homeworld of Maridun, and the Lurmen "roll up" and propel themselves along the ground the same way the Amanin did in a tale from Dark Horse Comics. And while the Lurmen may not present the same bone-chilling threat as the reptiles who preceded them in storytellers' imaginations, they eventually prove pretty capable fighters in their own right.

## Aayla Secura

Twi'lek Jedi Aayla Secura's agility and athleticism make her one of the Jedi Order's deadliest fighters. She is also a mentor to young Jedi such as Ahsoka Tano.

## EPISODE HIGHLIGHT

I CAN'T LEAVE HIM! MASTER, I KNOW IF I WAS HURT, HE'D NEVER LEAVE ME BEHIND!

I KNOW THIS IS HARD, AHSOKA.

BUT ANAKIN HAS TO STAY BEHIND AND WE HAVE TO GO NOW. THERE'S NOTHING MORE WE CAN DO FOR HIM.

## LANGUAGE LESSONS

As the Jedi cruiser speeds toward Maridun, the Aurebesh on the cockpit readout warns of IMPACT.

## ALIEN PROFILE
### Mastiff Phalones

The giant, vicious avians known as mastiff phalones are native to Maridun, where they prowl the grasslands in packs. They are descended from flying creatures, but evolution long ago turned their wings into powerful limbs tipped with terrible claws.

## PLANET PROFILE
### Quell

**Region:** Outer Rim

**Inhabitants:** Various

The deep blue world of Quell is one of many remote worlds with the poor luck to become a battleground between Separatist and Republic forces, who duel high in the planet's skies.

## IMPOSSIBLE THINGS

To find the right look for Maridun and the Lurmen's seed-pod village, Dave Filoni's team was influenced by everything from Dark Horse Comics to Ralph McQuarrie paintings to the work of the classic American illustrator N.C. Wyeth. But knowing what Maridun should look like was one thing—bringing it to life amid the demands of production was something else entirely.

# Tee Watt Kaa

An elder of the Lurmen's Te Padka faith, Tee Watt Kaa is a devout pacifist who has led his followers across to galaxy to Maridun in an effort to escape the Clone Wars.

"It is very difficult to create a planet like Maridun," says Filoni. The problem, he says, is one of complexity: Increasing the complexity of the visuals may limit other parts of production, such as how many shots can be done or how many characters can be used.

Luckily, he says, "we have very talented teams here and overseas," adding that "sometimes it's very difficult, but there's been nothing that we've been tasked with that we haven't been able to overcome."

Such difficulties are nothing new for *Star Wars*, he notes—the classic trilogy began with the need to create a convincing starfighter attack on a giant space station, while the prequels had digital characters such as Watto and Jar Jar Binks interacting with actors.

## DROID PROFILE

### Rocket Super Battle Droid

Super battle droids are tough but frustratingly slow for Separatist commanders who want to throw them at Republic forces. The B2-RP battle droid is designed to address this weakness, allowing the droids to fly to the fight and engage the enemy.

## EPISODE HIGHLIGHT

HEY, KID!

I KNOW! I KNOW! I'M HANGING ON!

## EPISODE HIGHLIGHT

GENERAL?
ARE YOU ALL
RIGHT?

BE ...
BE ... HIND ...
YOU ...

## IMPOSSIBLE THINGS (cont'd)

"Everyone who's worked on *Star Wars* has been asked to do impossible things," Filoni says, adding, "In *Clone Wars* I believe we are following in the footsteps of those great artists that came before us, to challenge ourselves to say, 'This hasn't been done on television before—especially with animation—but we want to do it. We're not going to let that hold us back. We're going to push forward, and no matter what George asks us to do—no matter how intimidating or crazy it seems in the beginning—we are going to figure out a way to do it.'"

### Tactical Droid

In an effort to turn the tide of the war, the Separatists have begun deploying tactical droids to lead units into battle. Tactical droids are emotionless, collecting relevant data about enemy units, and computing odds to determine the ideal strategy for the battlefield.

# GALACTIC DISPATCHES
## WITNESS TO THE JEDI

Wullf Yularen grew up on Anaxes, the son of a legendary instructor who was famous for expecting his cadets to perform equally flawlessly whether countering a Marg Sabl maneuver or selecting the right utensils throughout an eleven-course Axumi banquet.

Wullf followed him into naval service; given command of an Outer Rim patrol, he rousted slavers on the lawless Listehol Run and destroyed pirate nests in Wild Space. As a captain in the Kwymar Sector Fleet, he became obsessed with improving operational security and ferreting out corruption. The Senate and the law-enforcement ministries were full of leaks, and many missions failed because the targets were tipped off.

Yularen's obsession eventually led him to resign his naval rank for a position in the Senate Intelligence Bureau, where his work brought him powerful enemies in the Senate and in the Bureau—who forced him into an early retirement on Anaxes.

Supreme Chancellor Palpatine noticed his efforts, however. When the Clone Wars began, Palpatine told Yularen that the Republic needed him. Yularen accepted a place in the new Republic Navy; promoted to admiral, he was assigned to the *Resolute*, Anakin Skywalker's Jedi Cruiser.

Yularen was awed by Anakin's abilities and his absolute faith in himself. But he was appalled that the young Jedi routinely ignored orders and took huge security risks. For all their powers, Yularen saw, the Jedi did nothing to improve operational security—in fact, they made it worse by following a separate chain of command not always responsive to Coruscant's orders. Yularen came to see that his work was far from done.

## Episode 14:

YOU ARE NOW UNDER THE PROTECTION OF THE SEPARATIST ALLIANCE. I CONGRATULATE YOU ON YOUR GOOD FORTUNE.

**Original Airdate:** 1/23/09

**Written by** Bill Canterbury

**Directed by** Steward Lee

**Cast**
Matt Lanter:
    Anakin Skywalker
Ashley Eckstein:
    Ahsoka Tano
George Takei:
    Lok Durd
Alec Medlock:
    Wag Too
George Coe:
    Tee Watt Kaa
Jennifer Hale:
    Aayla Secura
Dee Bradley Baker:
    Clone troopers
Matthew Wood:
    Battle droids
Corey Burton:
    Count Dooku
Tom Kane:
    Narrator

# DEFENDERS OF PEACE

"When surrounded by war, one must eventually choose a side."

## SYNOPSIS

As Anakin is healing, Rex spots a Separatist ship heading toward the planet. Separatist general Lok Durd announces that the village is under protection from the Separatists—and then orders the droids to ransack it. Durd has a weapon, the defoliator capsule, which is designed to destroy only organic matter, but leave machinery unharmed. The Jedi convince the Lurmen to fight for their home and, together, they stop Durd and destroy the defoliator.

## NEWSREEL

Republic forces in retreat! While rescuing General Aayla Secura from certain defeat, Anakin Skywalker has been seriously injured. After a narrow escape, our heroes crash-landed on the remote world of Maridun. Stranded, and with no way to contact the Republic, the Jedi receive medical aid from the peaceful Lurmen colonists. But even on this tiny planet, the war threatens to follow the Jedi.... ■

**Cast (Continued)**
David Acord:
    Pune Zingat

**Location:** Maridun

**Vehicles:** Armored assault tank, C-9979 landing craft, Neimoidian shuttle, *Venator*-class Star Destroyer

**Weapons:** DC-15A blaster rifle, DC-15S blaster, E-5 blaster rifle, DC-17 hand blaster, defoliator capsule, lightsaber

## NEVER MIND THE GAP

George Takei, who played Mr. Sulu in a certain other venerable science-fiction franchise, supplies the voice of the Neimoidian general Lok Durd in "Defenders of Peace." Dave Filoni had crossed paths with Takei before, on *Avatar: The Last Airbender*—in the 2005

## CHARACTERS

Commander Bly
Count Dooku
Lok Durd
Tee Watt Kaa
Captain Rex
Aayla Secura
Anakin Skywalker
Ahsoka Tano
Wag Too
Tub
Pune Zingat
Yoda

## Pune Zingat

Lok Durd's chief weapons technician is Pune Zingat, an Aqualish, whose careful planning and design work have much to do with the Neimoidian's success.

## DROID PROFILE
### Recon Droid

Hovering recon droids come in a number of shapes and sizes, and are programmed to sneak behind enemy lines and use their finely-honed sensors to spy on Republic officers' conversations.

## NEVER MIND THE GAP (cont'd)

episode "Imprisoned," Takei plays the warden of a Fire Nation prison at sea. (Despite this, Filoni says they didn't actually meet until Takei showed up to work on *The Clone Wars*.) Filoni found Takei's turn on *Avatar* memorable—"he was really over the top, very funny"—and Lok Durd and his treatment of the Lurmen reminded Filoni of the role.

## EPISODE HIGHLIGHT

WHY ARE THEY TEARING APART OUR HOMES? WE'VE DONE NOTHING TO THEM!

VIOLENCE. THAT'S WHAT THOSE DROIDS ARE PROGRAMMED FOR.

So he and some other veterans of that show looked for a way to bring Takei aboard.

Still, Filoni is somewhat nonplussed by the idea that Sulu's presence on Maridun is some kind of epochal science-fiction moment.

"I guess to a lot of people on the crew it was a big deal because he's from *Star Trek*, not *Star Wars*," Filoni says. "I keep being told he's bridging this gap. I guess there's some gap there that I don't really know about. But a lot of the crew got a kick out of that, and a lot of people have since. So that's exciting."

## REMEMBERING THE FUTURE

At one point in "Defenders of Peace," Aayla Secura risks her life to rescue

## WEAPON PROFILE
### Defoliator

Lok Durd's latest invention is the defoliator capsule, a missile that kills all living matter within its blast radius but leaves machinery such as battle droids—intact.

## EPISODE HIGHLIGHT

UH, SHOULD WE TAKE COVER?

NO, IDIOT. IT'S NOT EVEN GOING TO HIT US.

## Lok Durd

An arrogant Neimoidian weapons researcher, Lok Durd is cruel and ambitious. He thinks nothing of testing his latest weapon on a peaceful Lurmen colony, hoping success will send him higher up the Separatist chain of command.

## ALIEN PROFILE

### Aqualish

The Aqualish have long resisted Republic authority, launching numerous uprisings in their galactic neighborhood. During the Clone Wars, the planet secedes from the galaxy and supports the Separatist cause.

## DROID PROFILE

### Super Battle Droid

B2 battle droids are big, tough, and dumb—and so aggressive they sometimes shove other Separatist droids out of the way as they stomp into combat.

## REMEMBERING THE FUTURE (cont'd)

Bly from a Trade Federation wall of fire. It's a thrilling moment—but once viewers catch their breath, they may find themselves remembering that in *Revenge of the Sith*, Bly shoots Aayla in the back. Viewers know what Aayla cannot—that the clones will unthinkingly obey the orders of Supreme Chancellor Palpatine, and work together to murder the Jedi generals with whom they have served and formed friendships. It isn't just Bly and Aayla, of course: Cody will order his troops to open fire on Obi-Wan Kenobi, Gree will attempt to kill Yoda, and Thire will hunt for Yoda in the Senate Chamber after the Jedi Master's duel with the newly declared Galactic Emperor. The future may be in motion during the Clone Wars, as it always is, but *Star Wars* fans know how it will unfold, and what disaster awaits the Jedi Order.

That may be in the audience's mind, but Henry Gilroy says he keeps obvious foreshadowing out of the scripts.

In *Star Wars* storytelling, he says, "the characters always stay in the moment. There's an immediacy to every situation that propels the stories forward—there are no flashbacks in *Star Wars*, and rarely any flash-forwards."

## EPISODE HIGHLIGHT

Regarding the Jedi and clones, Gilroy says, "I never think about where their relationship is going except that at this point in the war they're fighting side by side, working together to save the Republic. The fact that

## Wag Too

A young Lurmen healer, Wag Too is the son of Tee Watt Kaa, and groomed by his father to lead the Maridun colony.

## ALIEN PROFILE

### Carrier Butterflies

Beautiful, brightly colored carrier butterflies are one of the few life-forms on Maridun that won't try to bite or claw you to death. Carrier butterflies are surprisingly intelligent: The Lurmen raise them from pupae and have taught them to convey simple messages.

## LANGUAGE LESSONS

The Aurebesh writing on the side of the shield generators that the Jedi and clones steal from the Separatists reads: CAUTION.

## REMEMBERING THE FUTURE (cont'd)

the Jedi and clones will save each other many times during the series is chillingly ironic on its own, considering how tragically things end up."

## Tub

A young Lurmen and friend of Wag Too's, Tub is one of the colony's best scouts. He is able to move through Maridun's grasslands speedily and silently.

# GALACTIC DISPATCHES
## ESCAPING THE WAR

For generations, some of Mygeeto's devout Lurmen have followed the code of Te Padka, refusing to harm others even in the face of death. In the decades before the Clone Wars, the Te Padka watched anxiously as disorder spread throughout the galaxy. The Republic wasn't at war, but the faithful sensed it was coming—and with Mygeeto near several strategic systems, they would be caught in the middle.

Several years before the Battle of Geonosis, a group of Te Padka left Mygeeto and settled on Maridun, a green world in a wild, largely unsettled part of the Outer Rim. It was far from the major trade routes, and thus an unlikely prize in any war.

It also had one of the galaxy's more dangerous ecosystems: Tribes of semi-sentient bipeds called Amanin claimed portions of the savannas, and their braves proved themselves by hunting the ferocious mastif phalones, fierce predators the size of banthas.

Even Maridun's hecont trees could be dangerous: They derived nourishment in part from proteins. The trees sprouted from underground runners, which could sense vibrations overhead, signaling the tree to drop massive seedpods in hopes of crushing its prey for the runners to feed on.

Carnivorous trees, Amanin warriors, and vicious predators convinced most beings to keep far away from Maridun. But the Te Padka leader Tee Watt Kaa thought the savage planet was perfect: What better way to prove the power of Te Padka than to live in peace in the midst of so hostile an environment?

# Episode 15:

LISTEN HERE, YOU SAVAGE: THIS WORLD BELONGS TO THE MOON OF PANTORA.

# TRESPASS

"Arrogance diminishes wisdom."

## SYNOPSIS

Republic gunships arrive on the ice-covered planet of Orto Plutonia to find an empty base and a row of clone helmets on pikes. Pantorian Chairman Cho, whose moon controls this world, blames the Separatists and believes that they are building a secret base to attack Pantora. Obi-Wan and Anakin come across the Talz village. Cho tells the Talz leader, Thi-Sen, that he will not leave Orto Plutonia and declares war on the Talz. Cho is wounded before Senator Chuchi is given the authority to negotiate peace with the Talz.

**Original Airdate:** 1/30/09

**Written by** Stephen Melching

**Directed by** Brian Kalin O'Connell

**Cast**
James Arnold Taylor:
    Obi-Wan Kenobi, Pantoran Assembly Representative
Matt Lanter:
    Anakin Skywalker
Brian George:
    Chairman Cho
Jennifer Hale:
    Senator Chuchi
Dee Bradley Baker:
    Thi-Sen, clone troopers
Anthony Daniels:
    C-3PO
Tom Kane:
    Narrator
Matthew Wood:
    Battle droids
Robin Atkin Downes:
    Pantoran guard

# NEWSREEL

Republic outpost, overrun! The Jedi have lost all contact with the clone security force stationed on the bleak, snow-covered planet of Orto Plutonia. Obi-Wan Kenobi and Anakin Skywalker, accompanied by dignitaries from the nearby moon of Pantora are sent to investigate the disappearance of the clone troopers on the desolate and forbidding landscape.... █

**Location:** Orto Plutonia

**Vehicles:** BARC speeder, CK-6 swoop (Freeco bike), Republic attack gunship, *Resolute* (*Venator*-class Star Destroyer)

**Weapons:** DC-15S blaster, DC-15A blaster rifle, DC-17 hand blaster, Talz spear, Talz club, Pantoran blaster

## CHARACTERS

C-3PO
Chairman Chi Cho
Senator Riyo Chuchi
Obi Wan Kenobi
R2-D2
Captain Rex
Thi-Sen
Anakin Skywalker

## DRESSING FOR THE COLD

Obi-Wan, Anakin, and the clone troopers take to the frozen surface of Orto Plutonia in cold-weather gear that may leave longtime *Star Wars* fans with a familiar feeling: Haven't they seen these outfits before? Say, on the plains of Hoth in *The Empire Strikes Back*?

"It's always fun when you have a character to put them in a new costume for a specific environment," Dave Filoni says. "They couldn't just walk around in their Jedi outfits, so we thought,

# Senator Chuchi

Young Riyo Chuchi disagrees with Chairman Cho's hostility and inflexibility, but can't think of a way to overrule her fellow Pantoran and avert a war with the Talz.

## DRESSING FOR THE COLD (cont'd)

'Let's make some Jedi snow gear. And let's base it on the jacket we like that Han Solo wore—but it's not going to be exactly that jacket.''

It won't be the only costume change for Obi-Wan and Anakin. Filoni says, "They're not always going to have the armor over their Jedi outfits—they're going to move into the tunics and tabards they wear in *Revenge of the Sith* eventually.''

As for the clone troopers' armor, Filoni says the design team was trying to show something that looked older than the

### TRIVIA

The snow gear worn by the clone troopers on Orto Plutonia is derived from early Ralph McQuarrie designs created for the snowtroopers in *The Empire Strikes Back.*

snowtroopers' armor in Empire and the similar-looking gear worn by the Galactic Marines in Episode III.

"They are inspired very much by Ralph McQuarrie's original snowtrooper designs that you see in very early *Empire Strikes Back* paintings," he says. "They have symbols painted on their helmets, there are numbers just like Ralph was trying to do. Again, we were able to mix a lot of classic *Star Wars* iconography into these episodes. And then not surprisingly, I think that someone my age would say, 'Wow, that feels like *Star Wars*.' Visually, we were able to put a lot of cues in for people to grab onto."

(By the way, Filoni says Han's jacket is brown.)

## Chairman Cho

Chi Cho has zealously defended Pantora for decades, and now sees anyone who disagrees with him as an enemy of his beloved people.

## PLANET PROFILE
### Orto Plutonia

**Region:** Outer Rim

**Inhabitants:** Talz

The Pantorans have declared that the frozen world of Orto Plutonia is their property. But for their claim to be accepted under Republic law, Orto Plutonia must be devoid of intelligent native life—and the Talz seem to have been there for many years.

## VEHICLE PROFILE
### Freeco Bikes

**Model:** CK-6 Swoop

**Class:** Speeder bike

**Weapons:**
• Laser cannons

## ALIEN PROFILE
### Pantorans

Blue-skinned near-humans, Pantorans are believed to be an offshoot of the Inner Rim's Wroonians. They fear their remote world will be the next target of the Separatist military machine.

## ALIEN PROFILE
### Talz

White-furred, four-eyed bipeds with sharp claws, the Talz are technologically primitive, but cunning warriors. They are native to Alzoc III, but a colony has lived on frigid Orto Plutonia for thousands of years.

## THE OLD WAYS

When Obi-Wan and Anakin are negotiating with the Pantoran dignitaries over how to approach the Talz, you're seeing the way life used to be for the Jedi, says Dave Filoni.

"You hear a lot of political talk about the Jedi's place versus the Senate's place and who orders who and who's in charge," he says. "This episode then becomes a look into the way the Jedi operated prior to the war. Yes, they're commanding clone troopers. Yes, this episode takes place during the war. But you see Anakin and Obi-Wan acting in much more of a diplomatic function than we've seen."

The role, Filoni says, is much like the one Qui-Gon Jinn plays on Naboo, telling Queen Amidala that he and Obi-Wan can only protect her, not fight a war for her.

"This is the role they've given up, largely, and replaced with being more militant," he says. "They're changing. It was a good way to show the past of the Jedi and the way they think—or at least Obi-Wan thinks—they'll act in the future."

## TOGETHER AGAIN

During the Clone Wars, C-3PO serves Padmé Amidala while R2-D2 is on the front lines with Anakin. It's a frustrating situation for the Jedi and

the Senator, who are secretly married. But it's also frustrating for the writers, who mostly have to keep R2 and 3PO apart.

"Their teaming up is a huge part of *Star Wars*," Henry Gilroy says. "Whenever we have a story where Padmé gets involved in the action with Anakin, as in the '*Malevolence*'

## Snow Gear

On Orto Plutonia, the clone troopers under Rex's command must wear rebreather hoods and thick thermal suits for protection from the bone-chilling cold. While necessary for survival, the extra gear restricts their movements in battle.

NOW THAT YOU HAVE CREATED PEACE BETWEEN YOUR PEOPLE AND THE TALZ . . .

REMEMBER ONE CRUCIAL THING.

YES, MASTER KENOBI?

MAKE IT LAST, SENATOR. MAKE IT LAST.

## TOGETHER AGAIN (cont'd)

climax, there's a good chance we'll have a 'droids' pairing. For 'Trespass,' it was George who brought Threepio into the mix as Anakin's translator, with much success."

Frustrated by the two's separation? Take heart: Gilroy says that "story ideas featuring Artoo and Threepio together are being written for later episodes."

## Thi-Sen

The Talz chieftain, Thi-Sen, known as the "Son of the Suns," was born amid omens of greatness, and must prove himself by defending his people against new invaders.

# GALACTIC DISPATCHES
## A MATTER OF LAW

The Pantoran Assembly's Chairman Cho thought Orto
Plutonia's Talz were savages who didn't deserve the rights of
sentient beings in Republic space—a claim Obi-Wan Kenobi
knew wouldn't hold up under Republic law. The Convention of
Civilized Systems offered a number of tests for determining
sentience, from tool use and social complexity to the ability to
communicate advanced concepts with other species. By those
tests, the Talz were clearly sentient.

Standard protocol for first contact is to send images of a
species to Republic authorities. If Obi-Wan had been able to
do that, he would have learned that the Talz also inhabit the
primitive world Alzoc III—and occasionally have been seen
in the wider galaxy. That would seem to undermine the Talz
claim to Orto Plutonia, but the Arquata Station Amendments
to the Convention of Civilized Systems covered sentient species
that lived in multiple systems but didn't appear capable of
interstellar travel—a classification that covered everything
from colonies descended into barbarism to populations
"seeded" by other species, such as the Arkanians or the
ancient Rakata. (Ironically, the Pantorans are themselves
believed to be an offshoot of the Wroonian species. )

Many previously unknown sentient races found in inconvenient
places were quietly exterminated, with their killers covering up
the dreadful crime so the Republic would never find out. With
Republic representatives present, Cho couldn't do that. But he
could lean on Senator Chuchi to order a confrontation with the
Talz, provoking a conflict he hoped would leave the colonists
dead and a few legal problems to be cleared up later. But
Cho had underestimated both Chuchi's morals and the Talz's
abilities.

# Episode 16:

*I REALLY WISH YOU HADN'T NOTICED THAT, SIR.*

# THE HIDDEN ENEMY

"Truth enlightens the mind, but won't always bring happiness to your heart."

**Original Airdate:** 2/6/09

**Written by** Drew Z. Greenberg

**Directed by** Steward Lee

**Cast**
Dee Bradley Baker:
   Clone troopers
James Arnold Taylor:
   Obi-Wan Kenobi, tactical
   droid
Matt Lanter:
   Anakin Skywalker
Nika Futterman:
   Asajj Ventress
Tom Kane:
   Narrator
Matthew Wood:
   Battle droids

**Location:** Christophsis

## SYNOPSIS

Building up to the events in the movie, Anakin and Obi-Wan realize that someone has been giving their plans to the Separatists when an ambush goes wrong and their secret location is swarmed by battle droids. As the Jedi investigate a Separatist base and are confronted by Ventress, Cody and Rex learn that the spy is one of their clones, Sergeant Slick.

## NEWSREEL

A planet under siege! Separatist forces mercilessly batter the beautiful and elegant world of Christophsis. Unable to defend themselves any longer, the people of Christophsis call upon the Jedi for assistance. Hoping to save lives and prevent further destruction, Obi-Wan Kenobi and Anakin Skywalker plan a daring ambush that can turn the tide in the fight for this crucial star system.... ∎

**Vehicles:** Armored Assault Tank, Republic attack gunship, BARC speeder, All Terrain Tactical Enforcer (AT-TE), C-9979 landing craft, Single Trooper Aerial Platform (STAP)

**Weapons:** Blaster cannon, DC-15A blaster rifle, DC-15S blaster, E-5 blaster rifle, DC-17 hand blaster, electrostaff, lightsaber

## CHARACTERS

Trooper Chopper
Commander Cody
Trooper Gus
Trooper Hawk
Trooper Jester
Obi-Wan Kenobi
General Whorm Loathsom
Trooper Punch
R2-D2
Captain Rex
Trooper Sketch
Anakin Skywalker
Sergeant Slick
Asajj Ventress

## TIMING IS EVERYTHING

Dave Filoni knows that longtime *Star Wars* fans are eager to know how the events of *The Clone Wars* fit in with the many tales of that conflict that have been told in comics and video games so far—and while he's not ready to tell all, he says "The Hidden Enemy" offers clues.

"It really is an anthology of tales set over the period of time that is the Clone Wars," Filoni says, adding

## Chopper

The clone nicknamed Chopper is a bit strange—he takes battle-droid fingers as war trophies. That's against the rules, but does it make him a traitor?

## PROFILE

### 501ˢᵗ Legion

An elite unit of clone troopers led by Captain Rex under the command of Jedi General Anakin Skywalker.

## EPISODE HIGHLIGHT

## TIMING IS EVERYTHING (cont'd)

that while episodes connected in arcs obviously fit together in that timeline, it's not necessarily true that one arc follows another just because it was shown later in the series. And in the meantime, he says, just relax and enjoy the story.

"All you need to know at this point is that 'The Hidden Enemy' is a prequel to *The Clone Wars* movie," he says. "Anakin and Obi-Wan are back on Christophsis, and it's an episode that kind of explains why they're in so much trouble at the beginning of the movie."

For fans who just can't let go of timeline worries, Filoni suggests letting Ahsoka be their guide. As one marker to where an episode fits chronologically, he suggests "A, if she's there or not—that usually gives you an idea of where this is happening in the war—and B, her attitude. How much of a brat is she? How disrespectful is she, versus how much she's learned? She's always a good barometer for where you're at."

## VEHICLE PROFILE

### Single Trooper Aerial Platform

**Model:** Starhawk speeder bike

**Class:** Airspeeder

**Weapons:**
• Blaster cannons

## THE BONDS OF WAR

Sergeant Slick has harsh words for the Jedi when he's captured, accusing them of enslaving the clones. It's an argument that's raised at various points in *The Clone Wars*, but Henry Gilroy notes that another relationship between the Jedi and clone troops is explored in "The Hidden Enemy."

"We get a sense of the bond and trust forming between the Jedi and clones in this story," he points out. "Anakin and Obi-Wan go off on their mission, having faith that Cody and Rex will get the job done and find the traitor in their ranks—which they do."

So what does Gilroy think of Slick's argument? Have the Jedi indeed enslaved the clone troops? Should they worry that the Jedi Order now leads men into battle who were created in vats to fight machines, and die doing so? Is that a betrayal of the Jedi vow to serve as keepers of the peace?

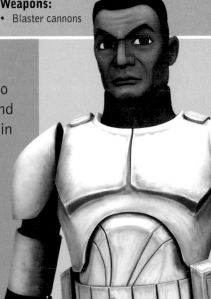

## Sergeant Slick

The veteran clone officer Sergeant Slick is actually a Separatist agent, infuriated at what he sees as the enslavement of his fellow clones by the Republic.

## THE BONDS OF WAR (cont'd)

"The Jedi are fully aware that it is immoral that an army of living beings has been created to fight a war, and die if necessary," he says. "Unfortunately, the galaxy is being torn apart, so the Jedi have no choice—they have been thrust into this role as warriors and must accept the help of the clones if they are to save the Republic. Just like soldiers in today's world, most clones are satisfied to do their duty and fight for their side."

*Star Wars* is make-believe, of course. But that's not to say that the stories told in *The Clone Wars* have no relation to the the world around us today: Storytellers have always pondered the latest headlines and used them to enrich and inform the tales they tell.

Gilroy notes that George Lucas "had a big part in developing this story to reflect the world today. I think he wanted to communicate the idea that some clones (or soldiers) might resent fighting a war they think is unjust, and explore

the idea of how far one clone (or soldier) might go to make a statement against it."

## THE BEAST

One of the odder characters in an episode full of clones who seem a bit odd is Chopper, the scarred clone caught collecting battle-droid fingers. As scripted, Chopper had more screen time—the episode opened with Cody, Slick, and Slick's platoon preparing for combat, while Chopper tried to program a small droid nicknamed "the Beast" to lead the battle droids into an ambush. Chopper seems weirdly

**LANGUAGE LESSONS**

Clone Trooper Sketch's tattoo is an Aurebesh S.

## Punch and Sketch

As clones in Slick's platoon, Punch and Sketch are suspected of being Separatist agents. But the two have a good alibi—they were in the base's mess hall.

## VEHICLE PROFILE
### BARC Speeder

**Model:** Biker Advanced Recon Commando speeder

**Class:** Speeder bike

**Weapons:**
- Laser cannons

## THE BEAST (cont'd)

attached to the sabotage droid, and casually rude to his commanding officer—a preview of his attitude when confronted in the barracks later.

In the script, the clones retreat after the Beast fails to work—and Dave Filoni did much the same. "At the end of the day, I just didn't understand why the clones would use a droid to attack droids," he says. "The whole point was you had clones to do that. So my editor, Jason Tucker, and I just cut it out."

# Whorm Loathsom

A general from the planet Kerkoidia, the ruthless Whorm Loathsom has won the respect of Coruscant's strategists for his repeated victories over Republic forces.

# GALACTIC DISPATCHES
## A WHORM WITH NINE LIVES

"The Hidden Enemy" takes place before *The Clone Wars* movie — but Obi-Wan Kenobi might still meet General Loathsom again.

After his capture on Christophsis, Whorm Loathsom was taken to Coruscant and swiftly found guilty of treason — the Republic still considered Kerkoidia a member world, and Loathsom's service in its planetary forces made him a member of the Republic military.

Once Republic Intelligence extracted all useful information from him, he was packed off to solitary confinement on the prison world of Akrit'tar.

Not long after Christophsis, Admiral Kreuge rebounded from his defeat at Salvara to take Kerkoidia, whose grand dukes immediately proclaimed renewed loyalty to the Republic and deep regret for their fling with Separatism. All that was history now, and dwelling on the past would be counterproductive.

The Kerkoidens did have suggestions for the best way to restore friendly relations and make sure no rogue Kerkoidens kept fighting — which would be unfortunate with the clone armies and the Jedi needed on the front lines. The Republic offered amnesty to most Kerkoiden fighters, with exceptions made for high-ranking Separatist officers and particularly outspoken nobles. And even they were permitted to serve their sentences in Kerkoiden custody.

Whorm Loathsom traded his Republic cell for house arrest in a rustic but still elegant castle in the Kerkoiden outback. Weeks after the transfer, Separatist operatives raided the castle and spirited him away. The Kerkoidens were deeply apologetic — despite their best efforts, some backward-thinking citizens still wanted to make trouble. Surely the Republic understood that — and wouldn't let unfortunate incidents like the escape of a lone Separatist risk further hard feelings.

# Episode 17:

WONDERFUL SPECIMENS!

# BLUE SHADOW VIRUS

"Fear is a disease; hope is its only cure."

## SYNOPSIS

Padmé and Jar Jar are captured by evil scientist Dr. Nuvo Vindi after uncovering a secret lab developing the Blue Shadow Virus. Anakin and Ahsoka are sent to Naboo to stop Vindi before he can release the virus, which, if released, could lead to a galaxy-wide plague. Clone troopers, led by Rex, swarm the lab and deactivate the virus bombs, while Anakin captures a fleeing Vindi.

**Original Airdate:** 2/13/09

**Written by** Craig Titley

**Directed by** Giancarlo Volpe

**Cast**
Catherine Taber:
    Padmé Amidala
Matt Lanter:
    Anakin Skywalker
James Arnold Taylor:
    Obi-Wan Kenobi
Ashley Eckstein:
    Ahsoka Tano
BJ Hughes:
    Jar Jar Binks
Michael York:
    Dr. Nuvo Vindi
James Mathis III:
    Captain Typho
Dee Bradley Baker:
    Clone troopers
Anthony Daniels:
    C-3PO
Gwendoline Yeo:
    Peppi Bow

## NEWSREEL

Battle droids on Naboo! As the Separatist rebellion rages through the galaxy, even peaceful planets are threatened. Following the discovery of Separatist droids wandering the grassy wasteland, Naboo is once again on high alert. Fearing their home is facing another invasion, Senator Amidala and Representative Binks race to Naboo to assess the situation. Meanwhile, near the Gungan swamplands, an even graver threat is about to be discovered.... ■

## THE CHALLENGE OF THE FAMILIAR

*The Clone Wars* has shown us many strange worlds, from coral-covered Rugosa to crystalline Christophsis. But Naboo—familiar to *Star Wars* fans from Episode I: *The Phantom Menace*—was a particular challenge.

"The challenge with Naboo, oddly enough, is the blue sky and the green grass," Dave Filoni says. "I mean, it really looks like

**Cast (Continued)**
Phil LaMarr:
    Tactical droid
Tom Kane:
    Yoda, narrator
Matthew Wood:
    Battle droids
Jameelah McMillan:
    Queen Neeyutnee
David Acord:
    Assistant droid

**Location:** Naboo

**Vehicles:** Naboo yacht, Republic attack gunship, *Sheathipede*-class transport shuttle, Naboo scout carrier

**Weapons:** E-5 blaster rifle, virus bomb, lightsaber, DC-15A blaster rifle, thermal detonator, DC-17 hand blaster, ELG-3A blaster pistol

## CHARACTERS

Senator Padmé Amidala
Jar Jar Binks
Peppi Bow
C-3PO
Obi-Wan Kenobi
LEP-86C8
Naboo Guardsman
Queen Neeyutnee
R2-D2
Captain Rex
Anakin Skywalker
Ahsoka Tano
Captain Gregar Typho
Dr. Nuvo Vindi
Yoda

# Peppi Bow

A shaak herder from Naboo's swamplands, Peppi Bow is determined to discover the source of the waterborne disease that killed her animals.

## ALIEN PROFILE

### Shaaks

Naboo's humans and Gungans both prize these fat, dim herd beasts for their meat. Though stupid and often sluggish, shaaks' gentle natures are appreciated by their handlers.

## EPISODE HIGHLIGHT

## THE CHALLENGE OF THE FAMILIAR (cont'd)

Earth—a very utopian Earth, but Earth nonetheless. You do an episode on a different planet, a bizarre alien planet, and you can take more liberties. Here, you're doing grassy hills and blue skies, and everybody's got a reference point. It's a lot trickier for us."

"Blue Shadow Virus" has many new characters and environments—so many that production capabilities were stretched badly, with the city of Theed limited to a single wide shot and views inside the hangar. Happily, that hangar is now an iconic setting in the *Star Wars* saga. This is where we saw Qui-Gon Jinn and Obi-Wan Kenobi stride up to a squad of armed battle droids, confident that their Jedi abilities make up for being badly outnumbered. This is where we saw those same two Jedi confront the tattooed champion of the newly revealed

## EPISODE HIGHLIGHT

THERE'S A GOOD CHANCE WE'RE ABOUT TO DESTROY ALL LIFE ON THIS PLANET, INCLUDING THE SENATOR'S.

SO, YES. I'M ON EDGE. WHY AREN'T YOU?

I'M BETTER AT HIDING IT.

Sith. And this is where we saw Anakin Skywalker—soon to be known as the best star pilot in the galaxy—turn a starfighter's guns on the enemy and roar off into battle, with R2-D2 riding shotgun.

"It was a huge thrill, I have to say, to shoot in that hangar and to see characters where you know Qui-Gon and Obi-Wan face off against Darth Maul," Filoni says. "The same hangar. I mean, that's great."

## LEP-86C8

A Coachelle Automata servant droid, 86C8 seems like most LEP droids—little more than a cute plaything. But this little droid has a deadly toy.

## TRIVIA

The hallways in the Separatist base were nicknamed "disco hallways" by the production team, and meant to evoke a Cloud City passageway explored by Luke Skywalker during *The Empire Strikes Back*.

## ALIEN PROFILE
### Slug-Beetles

These bright blue insects dwell along the roots of the perlote trees found in Naboo's swamps. They are prized as delicacies by Gungans, who often go to considerable lengths to catch so tasty a snack.

## VEHICLE PROFILE

**Model:** Theed Hangars Scout Carrier

**Class:** Scout ship

**Weapons:**
• Laser cannons

## TAKE TWO ON NABOO

Henry Gilroy says that the story of "Blue Shadow Virus" came from George Lucas, "I believe because he wanted to go back to the worlds he had created in the films—he loves seeing his creations in the new animated medium."

Gilroy was happy to return to Naboo, but he wanted to make sure there were some new wrinkles awaiting fans.

"When I go back to those worlds, I always like to add more aspects to them—a new location or characteristic that expands the way we think about them to make them richer and more interesting," he says. "There is always the responsibility to be true to what came before, but also to make what's there feel fresh and new, too. For example, the Separatists have a hidden underground bioweapons lab. A lot of fans were curious how the lab got there, but it was actually constructed 11 years earlier when the Trade Federation occupied Naboo in *The Phantom Menace*."

## THE STARFIGHTER TRAP

In creating the virtual set for the Theed hangar and filling it with starfighters, Dave Filoni and his team accidentally recreated a *Star Wars* mistake.

"We had a problem with the Naboo starfighters, in putting them in their stalls—the tails on those things were so long that they kept bumping into the walls," Filoni says. "So if you look in the episode, we put a little donut there, like the tail is inserted into a little socket in the wall."

The donut was the best the team could do, Filoni says—the starfighters didn't

## Dr. Nuvo Vindi

Nuvo Vindi is as brilliant as he is dangerous—he loves the purity of viruses, and dreams of a galaxy ruled by viruses after all "higher" life has been destroyed.

**EPISODE HIGHLIGHT**

## PROFILE

### Blue Shadow Virus

A generation before the Clone Wars, a quarantine contained the Candorian plagues, and the Blue Shadow Virus responsible was eliminated from the galaxy. Or so scientists thought. Now, Dr. Vindi has brought the virus back and engineered it to be deadlier than ever.

## PLANET PROFILE

### Naboo

Ten years before the Clone Wars, Naboo was invaded by the Trade Federation. The efforts of a band of heroes including Padmé Amidala, Jar Jar Binks, Anakin Skywalker, and Obi-Wan Kenobi wrecked Nute Gunray's plans—and the Trade Federation Viceroy swore one day he would have his revenge

## THE STARFIGHTER TRAP (cont'd)

quite fit in the stalls and there wasn't enough time to make changes so they would. But the director was baffled by the problem: He knew his team had measured everything accurately.

So what had happened?

"I talked to [Industrial Light and Magic visual-effects whiz] John Knoll about this problem and he said, 'You know, we had the same problem in *Phantom Menace*.' And I thought, 'Oh my gosh.' I found that kind of fascinating. And I give a lot of credit to the design and modeling team—we walked into the same trap that they had in Episode I."

## Naboo Guardsman

The Royal Naboo Security Forces are charged with the defense of Naboo as well as serving as bodyguards for the ruling monarch and their court.

# GALACTIC DISPATCHES
## DISEASE VECTOR

As living beings, the Republic's clone troopers were vulnerable to diseases that wouldn't bother battle droids—and since the clones shared the same genetic blueprint, they should all be equally vulnerable to the same illnesses.

Separatist bioweapon researchers experimented with viruses specially tailored to the clones, breeding nanoviruses designed to attack beings with the clone troopers' genetic signature. One strain was released on Kamino by the treacherous Kuma Nai, who died before she was able to bring it to the Separatists. Others were spread by octuptarra tri-droids, earning them the nickname "virus droids."

Another line of research focused on hive viruses, which could infect other living beings, too: A brain plague released on General Grievous's orders during the Battle of Loedorvia killed not just legions of clone troopers, but nearly every human in the Weemell Sector before an antidote was found.

The Loedorvian outbreak terrified the Core Worlds —and left Republic scientists frantically cataloguing known viruses and researching potential antidotes. One of the most frightening possibilities was that someone might weaponize a plague that had depopulated Candoria and its colonies two decades before the Clone Wars. It had been prevented from spreading only by a strict and ruthless quarantine. The pathogen responsible for the Candorian plague, which had periodically ravaged parts of the galaxy over the millennia, was nicknamed the Blue Shadow Virus, and had been studied by many researchers because it was so deadly to so many different species. But because it was so dangerous to all life, the Republic thought, not even the most ruthless Separatist researcher would dream of using it as a weapon.

# Episode 18:

JEDI OR NOT, NOBODY GETS OFF THIS ROCK ALIVE.

# MYSTERY OF A THOUSAND MOONS

"A single chance is a galaxy of hope."

**Original Airdate:** 2/13/09

**Written by** Brian Larsen

**Directed by** Jesse Yeh

**Cast**
Matt Lanter:
    Anakin Skywalker
Catherine Taber:
    Padmé Amidala, Angel
Ashley Eckstein:
    Ahsoka Tano
James Arnold Taylor:
    Obi-Wan Kenobi
Matthew Wood:
    Battle droids
James Mathis III:
    Captain Typho
Michael York:
    Dr. Nuvo Vindi
David Kaufman:
    Jaybo Hood
BJ Hughes:
    Jar Jar Binks
Phil LaMarr:
    Amit Noloff

## SYNOPSIS

The clones realize that one of the vials of the Blue Shadow Virus is missing from Vindi's lab. Before they can contain the last vial, Padmé, Jar Jar, Ahsoka, and Rex are all poisoned. Anakin and Obi-Wan head to the planet Iego to find the only known cure. However, Iego has problems of its own—it's surrounded by a network of laser stations programmed to shoot down any starship that tries to leave.

# NEWSREEL

Hard-pressed Jedi and their valiant clone troopers have thwarted an insidious Separatist plot to plant bombs loaded with the deadly Blue Shadow Virus in key Republic systems. Obi-Wan Kenobi and Anakin Skywalker have captured the vile scientist behind the nefarious scheme: Dr. Nuvo Vindi. Now the Jedi plan to transport Vindi to the Republic capital for trial.... ∎

## DOCTOR VINDI, I PRESUME

Dave Filoni calls the Separatist bioweapons researcher Dr. Nuvo Vindi "on the extreme end of *Star Wars* villains—he's one of those ones who's a bit absurd. But he's evil because of his absurdity."

George Lucas was very interested in having a big, boisterous performance for Dr. Vindi, which led to the casting of the veteran British actor Michael

**Cast (Continued)**
Tom Kane:
    Narrator

**Locations:** Naboo, Iego

**Vehicles:** *Sheathipede*-class transport shuttle, *Twilight* (G9 Rigger), Republic attack gunship

**Weapons:** DC-15S blaster, virus bomb, DC-17 hand blaster, E-5 blaster rifle, lightsaber

## CHARACTERS

Senator Padmé Amidala
Jar Jar Binks
Captain Rex
Jaybo Hood
Obi-Wan Kenobi
Amit Noloff
R2-D2
Anakin Skywalker
Ahsoka Tano
Captain Gregar Typho
Dr. Nuvo VIndi

## Captain Gregar Typho

A one-eyed veteran of the invasion of Naboo, Typho has sworn to protect Padmé Amidala against the next Separatist plot aimed at her.

## ALIEN PROFILE

### Xandu

Leathery-winged predators, xandu glide among Iego's peaks, hunting for unwary creatures they can snatch from cliffs and ledges.

## PLANET PROFILE

### Iego

**Region:** Outer Rim

Most think Iego is a legend, the cursed home of angels and marooned space pilots. As Obi-Wan and Anakin discover, these stories are true—from a certain point of view.

## DOCTOR VINDI, I PRESUME (cont'd)

York. *The Clone Wars* team had thought about York for different roles, including Admiral Yularen, but as Filoni notes, "we thought it would be really fun to have him try doing this very over-the-top character."

York saw Vindi as "a bit crazy, as if he's been in the lab too long," and then "just took it and ran with it," Filoni recalls. "When he says 'Yes yes yes yes yes' over and over and over I think it's really pretty funny." And indeed Vindi is funny, from the way he peers through his spectacles to the grand pronouncements he makes to his theatrical pauses of disbelief when his plans go awry, leaving him slack with disappointment. He's a mix of a slapstick antagonist from a cartoon and an evil mastermind from a spy thriller. Between York's vocal performance and the animators'

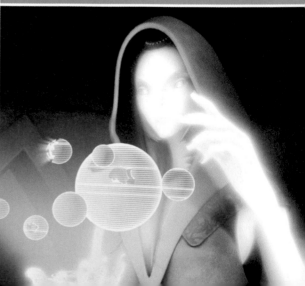

WHERE'S THE ANTIDOTE, VINDI?

HEHEHE. YOU MISTAKE MY ROLE, JEDI.

MY JOB WAS TO MANUFACTURE THE PLAGUE, NOT TO CURE IT.

inspiration, you find Vindi demands your attention.

But can a villain be funny? Sure, says Filoni, particularly since York brought an underlying menace to Vindi's craziness. He may seem comical when he's preaching about the perfection of viruses or sending a bunny droid on a secret mission, but he's absolutely serious about releasing a horrible disease into the galaxy, even if that means planets are swept clean of life.

## Amit Noloff

Once a successful spice merchant, the Quarren Amit Noloff has gone mad while marooned on Iego, and now tells all who will listen about the Curse of Drol.

## LANGUAGE LESSONS

The city of Cliffhold is full of Aurebesh graffiti. Look around and you'll find Jaybo Hood's name on several surfaces.

## ALIEN PROFILE

### Quarren

The Quarren have been rivals and occasional antagonists of the Mon Calamari for millennia, and some of their best starship engineers have pledged their loyalty and expertise to the Separatist cause.

## WEAPON PROFILE

### Drol

The ghost that imprisons Iego's population is actually a network of laser stations programmed to shoot down starships—a remnant of the days when the Separatists used Iego as a base.

## DOCTOR VINDI, I PRESUME (cont'd)

"Not every villain can be this total baddie like Vader or Darth Maul," Filoni says. "You need bizarre, eccentric, evil guys."

## GUNFIGHT AT THE IEGO CORRAL

According to Henry Gilroy, "Mystery of a Thousand Moons" is one of those *Clone Wars* episodes that changed a lot from the vision he and Dave Filoni originally had.

"It was more of a classic western where Anakin meets his match and has a ship-to-ship duel with this teenage character, like young gunfighters," he says, adding that "once Anakin beats the hotshot kid, he earns his respect and the kid helps the Jedi."

The duel didn't survive, but the character motivation did—Jaybo is initially dismissive of Anakin and Obi-Wan, but his opinion of the two Jedi changes after they survive their

quest for reeksa vines and their first encounter with Drol. Jaybo may still think trying to escape Iego is madness, but he's willing to help, and he gives Anakin and Obi-Wan a quartet of his tamed vulture droids in order to carry out their plan.

Gilroy says that "it was George himself who wanted to see Jaybo younger— and, I think, comment on what Anakin could have been had he stayed back on Tatooine."

Appropriately enough, therefore, Jaybo's final character design closely resembles early concept art of Anakin from production of *The Phantom Menace*. Imagine

## The Angels

Formally known as the Diathim, Iego's Angels are reputed to be the most beautiful creatures in the galaxy. Anakin Skywalker heard of them when he was a child on Tatooine—but never imagined they were real.

## EPISODE HIGHLIGHT

## ALIEN PROFILE

### Reeksa Vines

Iego's reeksa vines stretch from the dim bottoms of canyons to the sunny tops of the planet's crags. But travelers are warned not to touch them, for fear of a close encounter with the plants' razor-sharp thorns and snapping jaws.

## GUNFIGHT AT THE IEGO CORRAL (cont'd)

if some alternate-universe Anakin had somehow won his freedom from Watto and used his remarkable skills with machines to become an eccentric figure living on the fringes of Mos Espa, served by reprogammed droids. Better than being a slave, of course, but a waste considering what Anakin could have been.

The viewer doesn't learn what happens to Jaybo after the destruction of Drol, but Anakin's example has shown him that he's now free to make something more of his life.

## Jaybo Hood

A young Iegan with a gift for tinkering with droids, Jaybo Hood has made himself into a little despot served by reprogrammed Separatist droids.

# GALACTIC DISPATCHES
## DOMAIN OF ANGELS

For millennia, Iego was thought to be a myth—a world ringed by moons and home to angels, demons, and unlucky castaways who would never again escape to the starlanes.

In truth, Iego was hidden away in the glowing heart of a knot of nebulae known as the Extrictarium. Those few who found the planet and escaped told tales of glowing angels who intercepted ships, leaving tribes of shipwreck survivors to fend for themselves on a barren world—if they weren't eaten by an even stranger subterranean species.

Several decades before the Clone Wars, scouts finally charted a safe course through the Extrictarium and established a settlement on Iego—the town of Cliffhold was founded as a port for spice shipments, and settlers managed to grow exotic crops from Iego's thin soil. But the World of a Thousand Moons attracted few visitors, remaining the stuff of legend to most in the galaxy.

Unfortunately, the Separatist leadership knew of the planet, and saw Iego as a potential fortress that would be easy to defend if the war went against them. A Separatist flotilla drove the Angels—known on Iego as the Diathim—from the moon Millius Prime and established a web of automated defenses around the planet. The Separatists soon changed their plans and abandoned Iego, but they left the defenses in place. Once again, Iego was a planet of the marooned.

## Episode 19:

DID YOU TRAIN HER *NOT* TO FOLLOW ORDERS?

# STORM OVER RYLOTH

"It is a rough road that leads to the heights of greatness."

**Original Airdate:** 2/27/09

**Written by** George Krstic

**Directed by** Brian Kalin O'Connell

**Cast**
Ashley Eckstein:
    Ahsoka Tano
Matt Lanter:
    Anakin Skywalker
Dee Bradley Baker:
    Clone troopers
Corey Burton:
    Mar Tuuk
Matthew Wood:
    Wat Tambor, battle droids
Tom Kane:
    Admiral Yularen, narrator
James Arnold Taylor:
    Obi-Wan Kenobi
Terrence "TC" Carson:
    Mace Windu
Tim Brock:
    Medical droid TB-2

## SYNOPSIS

Anakin and Ahsoka must destroy the Separatist blockade around the planet of Ryloth so Obi-Wan can get his landing party to the planet's surface. Outgunned, Anakin devises a plan. Pretending that he is ready to surrender, the Jedi crashes an empty star destroyer into the Separatist battleship while Ahsoka leads the starfighters to finish the job.

# NEWSREEL

Manhunt! After a long and perilous search, the Jedi finally track down Separatist leader Count Dooku. During a heroic attempt to capture the count, Anakin Skywalker has gone missing. Having lost contact with Skywalker, Obi-Wan Kenobi heads toward his friend's last known location, a lone Separatist frigate in the far reaches of the Outer Rim.... ◼

**Location:** Ryloth

**Vehicles:** *Acclamator I*-class assault ship, Delta-7B *Aethersprite*-class starfighter, C-9979 landing craft, Republic attack gunship, *Lucrehulk*-class battleship, *Munificent*-class star frigate, *Nu*-class attack shuttle, V-19 Torrent starfighter, *Venator*-class Star Destroyer

## CHARACTERS

Pilot Axe
Obi-Wan Kenobi
Pilot Kickback
R2-D2
R7-A7
Captain Rex
Anakin Skywalker
Pilot Slammer
Pilot Swoop
Wat Tambor
Ahsoka Tano
Pilot Tucker
Mar Tuuk
Mace Windu
Admiral Wullf Yularen

## A PADAWAN'S LESSON

The battle over Ryloth teaches Ahsoka a painful lesson, as Dave Filoni notes. "Her training with Anakin over the months has made her quite confident in her abilities, and she is play-acting at being like Anakin," he says. "She sees his success, she sees his abilities, and she wants to be more like that. So she gets very headstrong and she stops listening to orders—like she sees

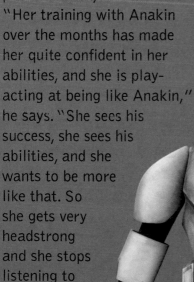

## Clone Pilot Axe

A capable clone trooper pilot, Axe normally served as Blue Leader, but hands his squadron over to Ahsoka Tano for the attempt to break the Ryloth blockade.

## ALIEN PROFILE

### Twi'leks

Twi'leks are graceful humanoids famous for their long brain-tails, known as lekku. They have been part of galactic society for millennia, but face extermination at the hands of the Separatists.

## VEHICLE PROFILE

### Trade Federation

**Model:** Modified *Lucrehulk* Cargo Freighter

**Class:** Capital ship

**Weapons:**
• Turbolasers, starfighter complement

## A PADAWAN'S LESSON (cont'd)

Anakin not always listening to Obi-Wan. The problem is that she's not ready."

In "*Shadow of Malevolence*," Anakin led the Y-wing attack on the *Malevolence* that got several of his pilots killed, and taught him that he's responsible for his men. "He's tried to teach that to Ahsoka, but she has not learned it—and now we see her making a very similar mistake," Filoni says. "She's getting herself in over her head, she's getting her men in over their heads, she's not listening to Admiral Yularen, and she's not listening to Anakin."

Ahsoka learns the hard way—by seeing most of her squadron shot down and knowing that she's

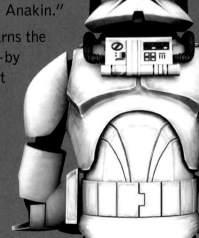

### Clone Pilot Kickback

As a member of Blue Squadron, clone pilot Kickback serves under Ahsoka Tano as Blue Four while attempting to liberate Ryloth from the Separatists.

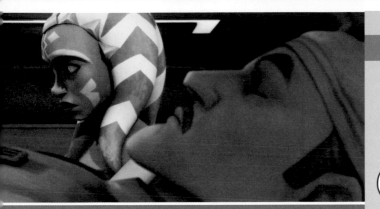

THIS IS MY FIRST TIME COMMANDING A SQUADRON, R7. LET'S MAKE A GOOD IMPRESSION.

WEET TOO WEET

OK, YOU BOYS READY?

THIS IS TWO, AXE, READY WHEN YOU ARE, SKIPPER.

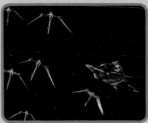

responsible for their deaths. "It's important for her to have to deal with that loss," Filoni says. "She has to deal with the consequences and the guilt that comes with causing these men to die."

## SWITCHING ROLES

Dave Filoni says "Storm Over Ryloth" gave the creative team the opportunity to have an ensemble cast of Jedi perform different military tasks on Ryloth. Anakin is in charge of breaking the blockade, while Obi-Wan has to fortify a landing position and knock out the Separatists' anti-aircraft guns—after which he and Mace Windu can retake Ryloth city by city.

Ahsoka's job is to lead a fighter squadron, with Anakin overseeing the effort from his Jedi cruiser's bridge. That may leave fans wondering why the Jedi would keep their best starfighter pilot on the sidelines.

"In the original script, Anakin was out there flying with Ahsoka," Filoni says. "But it seemed to take away from her story. It made it a lot harder to believe that they would get caught in a bad situation. In the end, George was the one who decided that Anakin shouldn't be out

SKYWALKER, WHAT TREACHERY IS THIS? YOU HAVE NOTHING TO BARGAIN WITH!

IN THAT CASE, I'LL BE GOING . . . OH, YOU CAN STILL HAVE MY SHIP.

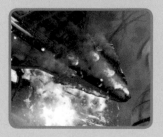

## SWITCHING ROLES (cont'd)

there flying—he should be on the bridge. He's a general, he needs to have some responsibility."

The decision opened up new storytelling possibilities: We see Ahsoka struggle with the demands of leading soldiers into combat, while Anakin wrestles with not being directly in the fight. "That gave us the opportunity to give both characters a chance to operate in a way we haven't seen from them," Filoni says.

## THE ONE THAT GOT AWAY

Mar Tuuk, the Neimoidian captain in charge of the Ryloth blockade, originally died at the culmination of Anakin's attack. And his death scene was a memorable one: Unable to escape an imminent collision with the *Defender*, the Neimoidian (named by Henry Gilroy after Dave Filoni's cat) calmly sat down in his command chair as a battle droid asked, "What should we do?"

Tuuk's answer: "We die."

The scene was an homage to *The Last Starfighter*, a Filoni favorite. But in the final version of the episode, Tuuk escapes, bucking the trend of speedy exits from new *Clone Wars* villains.

"At the end of the day, George really liked Mar Tuuk," Filoni says. "He thought, 'He's a great character—I don't want him to die.' So—for once—Mar Tuuk gets away. We actually reshot it just so he could live."

## ANAKIN'S TEACHINGS

Henry Gilroy sees Ahsoka's bitter lesson about the nature of war as a chance for Anakin to learn and grow as a teacher.

"At first, Ahsoka is so shaken by her failure that she's ready to give up," Gilroy says. "She even

## EPISODE HIGHLIGHT

IT WASN'T YOUR FAULT.

I LOST SO MANY OF MY PILOTS.

TAKE HEART, LITTLE ONE, THAT'S THE REALITY OF COMMAND.

## TRIVIA

Mar Tuuk's command chair and motorized eyepiece are nods to Lord Kril's gear in the 1984 movie *The Last Starfighter*.

## Mar Tuuk

A capable Neimoidian officer, Mar Tuuk oversees the Separatists' Ryloth blockade. He correctly predicts that Anakin Skywalker will return to the battle—but not how the Jedi will do so.

## VEHICLE PROFILE

### Escape Pod

**Model:** *Venator*-class Star Destroyer escape pod

**Class:** Lifeboat

**Weapons:**
• None

## PLANET PROFILE

### Ryloth

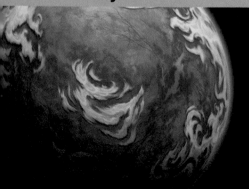

**Region:** Outer Rim

Ryloth has long been a source of slaves and spice, with Twi'leks sometimes decrying these cruel trades but as often profiting from them. Ryloth's strategic location and great wealth make it a Separatist target.

## ANAKIN'S TEACHINGS (cont'd)

believes she's lost the trust of the clones and Admiral Yularen, so she's at her lowest point. Recognizing this is a turning point for her, Anakin shows great restraint. He could have really laid into her about a mistake that cost many lives, but he realized to get her 'back on the horse' he would have to show patient compassion and—more importantly— trust in her."

Anakin's trust, Gilroy says, "ultimately raises her out of her self-pity and back into command, where she belongs. This was an important moment for Anakin as Ahsoka's master, too. In the past he would have tried to do it all himself and probably gotten killed. But in lifting Ahsoka up, he raised himself as well."

### R7-A7

R7-A7 serves as Ahsoka Tano's astromech during the strike on the Ryloth blockade. The droid is one of several in the Republic fleet with advanced prototype logical modules.

# GALACTIC DISPATCHES
## PLANET OF EXTREMES

Ryloth is a planet of great beauty but also extreme conditions, few more famous than those found in its equatorial deserts. There, blistering heat storms rise without warning to sweep across kilometers of land, and these furnacelike cyclones can kill an unprotected Twi'lek in seconds.

The heat storms are so famous that many tourists are surprised to find such conditions don't dominate the planet. Ryloth also has lush bands of terrain, such as the forest-dotted Cazne Plains where much of its population lives, and where the capital of Lessu attracts spacers from across the galaxy.

Ryloth's best-known exports give the planet a bad reputation. Slavery has been a Twi'lek industry for millennia, and Twi'lek dancing girls are common sights in crimelords' dens and wealthy nightclubs. Ryll spice is also common on Ryloth, and millions of credits move from the planet through the lawless reaches of the Outer Rim to Hutt Space and beyond.

Twi'leks hate it when people assume they're all dancers or smugglers, but Ryloth's rulers have never really tried to end slavery or the spice trade. Twi'leks like to keep their options open, whether it's how to make a living or how to keep out of a galactic civil war. As the proverb says, "One cannot defeat a heat storm, one must ride it." Unfortunately for the Twi'leks, their neutrality did them no good in the Clone Wars—the combination of Ryloth's strategic location on the Corellian Run and its spice wealth proved irresistible to Count Dooku.

# Episode 20:

NERRA. NERRA.

# INNOCENTS OF RYLOTH

"The costs of war can never be truly accounted for."

## SYNOPSIS

On the surface of Ryloth, Obi-Wan and Rex lead a small attack force to destroy Separatist proton cannons that are being protected by a shield of captive Twi'leks. Troopers Waxer and Boil find a small girl named Numa who leads them through a secret passage to the prisoners. Once the Twi'leks are free, Obi-Wan and the clones are able to destroy the proton cannons, allowing Mace Windu's invasion force to arrive.

**Original Airdate:** 3/6/09

**Written by** Henry Gilroy

**Directed by** Justin Ridge

**Cast**
Dee Bradley Baker:
    Clone troopers
James Arnold Taylor:
    Obi-Wan Kenobi
Corey Burton:
    TX-20, Nilim Bril
Matthew Wood:
    Wat Tambor, battle droids
Catherine Taber:
    Numa
Terrence "TC" Carson:
    Mace Windu
Tom Kane:
    Narrator

**Location:** Ryloth

# NEWSREEL

Invasion! Separatist leader Wat Tambor has taken control of the planet Ryloth and subjugated its people through a brutal droid occupation. In a daring surprise attack, Jedi Anakin Skywalker and his Padawan, Ahsoka Tano, defeated the space blockade guarding the planet. Now, Jedi generals Mace Windu and Obi-Wan Kenobi lead a massive invasion to liberate the starving people.... ∎

**Vehicles:** Armored Assault Tank (AAT), *Acclamator I*-class assault ship, Republic attack gunship, *Venator*-class Star Destroyer

**Weapons:** DC-17 blaster, DC-15A blaster rifle, E-5 blaster rifle, rocket launcher, electrostaff, lightsaber

## CHARACTERS

Trooper Boil
Nilim Bril
Commander Cody
Obi-Wan Kenobi
Numa
Wat Tambor
TX-20
Trooper Waxer
Mace Windu
Trooper Wooley

## THE HERSHEY BAR

The friendship between the clones Boil and Waxer and the Twi'lek refugee Numa made this episode an instant favorite among fans—but it's the latest version of a classic story with plenty of real-life equivalents.

"You hear stories from World War II about American soldiers finding kids in France or Italy and they give them a Hershey bar," says Dave Filoni. "They

## Waxer

Waxer, along with clone trooper Boil, serves under Commander Cody in the 212th Attack Battalion. They are sent to search a Twi'lek village for Separatist units.

I CALCULATE THE REMAINING CLONES ARE ATTEMPTING A DESPERATE FINAL OFFENSIVE.

THEIR CHANCES OF SUCCESS AGAINST US ARE 742 TO 1.

YOU HAD BETTER BE RIGHT.

I AM A DROID. I AM ALWAYS RIGHT.

## THE HERSHEY BAR (cont'd)

give them something to eat, a little token of kindness, something that is going to help them get through to the next day. One of the stories we knew we wanted to do was about the little kid lost in the war—that's a very real situation." Filoni says the story of Ryloth's recapture went through many revisions, becoming smaller in scale.

"It used to be a big Normandy, D-Day invasion," he says. "But in the end we changed it so that it was really about these more personal stories. And the little girl who was kind of in the background of an early version of the script really moved to the forefront. That changed the entire dynamic—how these clones interact with the populations they're saving and how they perceive them became a very important idea."

## BRINGING NUMA TO LIFE

At various points in "Innocents of Ryloth," we see Numa terrified, brave, and finally joyous at being reunited with her relatives.

"Kids can surprise you with what they're capable of," Dave Filoni says. "I think it's important to see the moment when she breaks down crying. It's like she's finally allowing herself to have these emotions—she finally goes back to her home because she's with these two soldiers and they're protecting her, so she feels vulnerable enough to express her emotions."

The animators, Filoni says, did a wonderful job "capturing this little child and her emotions. The first time Boil and Waxer take their helmets off and

## Boil

Along with clone trooper Waxer, Boil serves under Commander Cody in the 212th Attack Battalion. They are sent to search a Twi'lek village for Separatist units.

## ALIEN PROFILE
### Gutkurrs

Gutkurrs are fierce predators who use their insect-like claws to dig themselves into Ryloth's desert sands, where they ride out heat storms and wait for prey to ambush.

## WEAPON PROFILE
### Proton Cannon

These artillery units can fire projectiles high into the atmosphere. They can be controlled by a gunner or fighter using their own built-in droid brains.

## BRINGING NUMA TO LIFE (cont'd)

she looks at them, it's a little magic moment for me because she goes a little wide-eyed. They did a great job of bringing that little girl to life and making her fun—but also making her vulnerable."

## THROUGH CLONE EYES

Henry Gilroy wanted to put a twist on this episode's storytelling by exploring the relationship between Numa and the clone troopers "from the clones' point of view—they just want to do their duty and destroy the droids. They're unconcerned about the inhabitants until they encounter one, get to know her, then come to better understand the importance of the fight. I also had our people in Iraq in mind while writing this story, so it was kind of a shout-out to them as well—because I realize they've been put in a tough position and are trying to help an enslaved populace against evil forces. I hope that came through."

Gilroy notes that because Numa only speaks Twi'lek, the character had to come alive through physical acting.

"I must give all credit to our amazing director Justin Ridge for executing that to perfection," he says. "Part of the strength of the episode relies on the fact that Numa cannot communicate with the clones easily, which makes their bonding moments emotionally powerful—her words can't express what she's feeling, yet she still manages to deeply touch the clones."

**EPISODE HIGHLIGHT**

## Numa

A young Twi'lek, Numa has escaped capture by battle droids thanks to her ability to move quickly and quietly and her knowledge of the tunnels beneath her village.

## LANGUAGE LESSONS

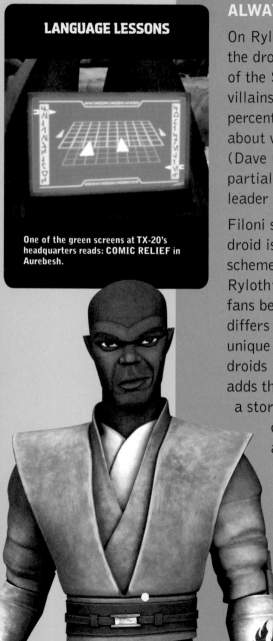

One of the green screens at TX-20's headquarters reads: COMIC RELIEF in Aurebesh.

## ALWAYS TELL THEM THE ODDS

On Ryloth, the Jedi and clones must face the droid commander TX-20. TX-20 is one of the Separatists' tactical droids, new villains who make cold calculations of percentages and ratios and keep data files about what individual Jedi do in battle. (Dave Filoni says the tactical droids are partially inspired by Lucifer, the Cylon leader from *Battlestar Galactica*.)

Filoni says we'll see that each tactical droid is unique, with its own voice, paint schemes, and colors. ("Innocents of Ryloth" isn't their first appearance for fans because the series' production order differs from its running order.) These unique characteristics make the tactical droids interesting as individuals, but Filoni adds that their introduction also solved a storytelling problem by giving the creators "an opportunity to have a villain that was smart but was disposable—that wasn't Dooku, that wasn't Ventress. So we didn't have to keep beating those guys. Grievous kept getting beaten early on in episodes and I really didn't like that. I think it takes away from him. We need to see him have more victories, not just always defeats."

# Mace Windu

A tough, no-nonsense member of the Jedi Council, Mace Windu is a terrible opponent for all those who would oppose the dictates of the Jedi Order.

# GALACTIC DISPATCHES
## THE TECHNO UNION

A thousand years before the Clone Wars, a number of the galaxy's industrial giants formed a guild, pledging to help each other restart factories and modernize production lines in order to rebuild a galactic economy shattered by war with the Sith. But the Techno Union soon changed, becoming a powerful lobby that intimidated independent companies and pushed the Senate for handouts and special legislation.

In the decades before the Clone Wars, the Techno Union followed the lead of the Trade Federation and demanded tax relief, privileged access to Outer Rim trade routes, and the right to build droid armies for self-defense. When the Separatists broke with the Republic, Techno Union foreman Wat Tambor allied the group with them. The Skakoan became a member of the Separatist Council, and called for all-out war against the Republic.

The huge number of Techno Union shipyards and factories made the Separatists a military force to be reckoned with. But some union members didn't agree with the Separatist cause, leading to a split in the guild. Some megacorps, such as Haol Chall Engineering and Baktoid Armor, agreed with Tambor. Others, such as BlasTech Industries and the Corellian Engineering Corporation, left the Union and swore loyalty to Coruscant. Some, such as Arakyd Industries, tried to remain neutral or supply arms to both sides. And a few—most notably TaggeCo.—initially aligned with the Confederacy but soon decided that had been a mistake. Such defections were crucial in allowing the Republic to build up its own fleets and armies.

## Episode 21:

YOU DON'T SURVIVE IN THE OUTER RIM BY BEING STUPID!

# LIBERTY ON RYLOTH

"Compromise is a virtue to be cultivated, not a weakness to be despised."

## SYNOPSIS

To defeat the Separatists on Ryloth and free the Twi'leks, Mace Windu enlists the aid of freedom fighter Cham Syndulla. With bombers destroying the Twi'lek villages, Windu leads his invasion team to the heavily protected Separatist headquarters. As Wat Tambor prepares to escape, the Republic and freedom fighters storm the base and bring an end to the occupation.

**Original Airdate:** 3/13/09

**Written by** Henry Gilroy

**Directed by** Rob Coleman

**Cast**
Terrence "TC" Carson:
   Mace Windu
Robin Atkin Downes:
   Cham Syndulla
Matthew Wood:
   Wat Tambor, battle droids
Dee Bradley Baker:
   Clone troopers
Matt Lanter:
   Anakin Skywalker
Phil LaMarr:
   Orn Free Taa
Corey Burton:
   Count Dooku, Gobi Glie
Ashley Eckstein:
   Ahsoka Tano
Tom Kane:
   Yoda, Admiral Yularen,
   narrator

# NEWSREEL

Republic victory is at hand! Clone troopers under the command of the Jedi have successfully invaded the Separatist-occupied world of Ryloth. Anakin Skywalker battles the enemy in the skies, while Obi-Wan Kenobi frees villages from the grip of vile Separatist leader Wat Tambor. Now Jedi General Mace Windu leads the attack on the enemy lines in the final offensive to liberate the capital city of Lessu.... ∎

## THE GREAT WINDU

The conclusion of the Ryloth arc gives us our first look at Mace Windu as a major character in an episode and he has some very memorable moments. He leads an army of clones and Twi'leks against the stronghold established by Wat Tambor in the city of Lessu, doing away with countless battle droids before apprehending the Separatist leader and ending Count Dooku's plot

## Wat Tambor

The Skakoan foreman of the Techno Union, Wat Tambor is named emir of occupied Ryloth, which he seeks to strip of its valuables.

**Cast (Continued)**
Ian Abercrombie:
    Chancellor Palpatine
James Arnold Taylor:
    Tae Boon
Gary Scheppke:
    TA-175

**Location:** Ryloth

**Vehicles:** All Terrain Tactical Enforcer (AT-TE), All Terrain Recon Transport (AT-RT), Armored Assault Tank (AAT), Republic attack gunship, Delta-7B *Aethersprite*-class starfighter, Multi-Troop Transport (MTT), BTL-B Y-wing starfighter, C-9979 landing craft, Single Trooper Aerial Platform (STAP), Hyena bomber

**Weapons:** Thermal blasters, DC-17 hand blaster, E-5 blaster rifle, lightsaber, DC-15S blaster, DL-44 blaster

## CHARACTERS

Tae Boon
Count Dooku
Gobi Glie
Chancellor Palpatine
Commander Ponds
R7-A7
Trooper Razor
Anakin Skywalker
Trooper Stak
Cham Syndulla
TA-175
Orn Free Taa
Wat Tambor
Ahsoka Tano
Mace Windu
Yoda
Admiral Wullf Yularen

## ALIEN PROFILE
### Skakoans

Skakoans evolved in a highly pressured methane atmosphere. When away from their home planet, they must wear protective suits and special breathing equipment.

## VEHICLE PROFILE
### Hyena Bomber

**Model:** Baktoid Self-Propelled heavy ordinance battle droid

**Class:** Bomber

**Weapons:**
• Laser cannons, concussion missiles

## THE GREAT WINDU (cont'd)

to enslave the Twi'lek planet. An impressive performance, to be sure, but Dave Filoni rejects the idea that Mace has any unusual powers—it's just that he's extremely focused and in tune with the Force.

Take the moment where the battle droids deactivate the bridge over the chasm that Mace and his clone troopers are crossing. Filoni gives credit to supervising sound editor Matt Wood and his team for a "great moment in sound"—the sound drops

down, "making it seem like you're in the focus of Mace Windu for that moment when he saves the clones and jumps off the bridge. Through sound we were able to take the audience and really put them into the mind of Mace Windu. He sees everything that slow, and with that kind of focus."

But that doesn't mean that Mace is a superhero, able to fly through the air or capable of superhuman feats of strength. Sure, he can use telekinesis to fling battle droids to their doom (and who wouldn't want to do that), but analyze his scenes carefully and you'll see that his most impressive moments rely on timing and awareness, as opposed to the benefits conveyed by midi-chlorians. In fact, Filoni compares Mace's gifts to those of athletes who could see the entire field while playing a sport, or who say the game seemed to move slowly for them.

## Commander Ponds

Formally known as CC-6454, Clone Commander Ponds serves Mace Windu, and regrets that service to the Jedi normally leaves him stuck on Coruscant, far from the front lines.

**EPISODE HIGHLIGHT**

**LANGUAGE LESSONS**

The back of Clone Commander Ponds's helmet says: SOME GUYS HAVE ALL THE LUCK in Aurebesh.

## VEHICLE PROFILE

### AT-RT

**Model:** All Terrain Recon Transport

**Class:** Walker

**Weapons:**
- Laser cannons

## THE GREAT WINDU (cont'd)

"There are people even within our own world who have the intuitiveness to go beyond," he says. "And that's what the Jedi do. They are trained to listen to the Force, to commune with the Force. They're feeling the presence of it and reacting and trusting their instincts."

## SAM I AM NOT

Mace Windu sure sounds like Samuel L. Jackson, but in the show his voice is actually provided by Terrence Carson.

You might know "TC" as Kyle Barker in *Living Single*, but he's also a veteran voice performer for video games, having appeared in the likes of EverQuest II and God of War. And he's provided Mace's pipes before, reading the character's lines in *The*

## TRIVIA

Look fast and you'll see battle droids carrying off the Ark of the Convenant as part of Wat Tambor's stolen stash. Will it be crated up in a warehouse somewhere on Skako?

## EPISODE HIGHLIGHT

THE REPUBLIC WILL HELP YOU REBUILD. WE WON'T ABANDON YOU.

YOUR TROOPS WILL STAY FOR SECURITY?

Clone Wars and Revenge of the Sith video games, as well as Battlefront II and Galactic Battlegrounds. (Kevin Michael Richardson has also voiced Mace in video games.)

"I always thought Mace had the potential to be this incredibly rich character when he does

FOR A WHILE. TO KEEP THE PEACE.

ANOTHER ARMED OCCUPATION IS NOT A FREE RYLOTH.

## Orn Free Taa

A Twi'lek Senator, the hopelessly corrupt Orn Free Taa spends most of his time on Coruscant, far from his ravaged homeworld.

HOW LONG BEFORE I AM FIGHTING YOU, MASTER JEDI?

## ALIEN PROFILE
### Blurrgs

Two-legged reptilian beasts, blurrgs are found on a number of worlds, from Endor to Ryloth. Twi'leks are skilled blurrg handlers, and ride the creatures into battle against the Separatists' droid armies.

## EPISODE HIGHLIGHT

GENERAL WINDU! PERHAPS WE CAN COME TO A COMPROMISE.

NOT WHEN I HOLD ALL THE CARDS.

### SAM I AM NOT (cont'd)

appear in stories—he brings all the best that the Jedi have to offer," Gilroy says. "Dave and I wanted to show that Mace is very powerful with the Force and a tremendous fighter. But he's a senior member of the Jedi Council because he's very wise and an accomplished diplomat. He knows the way to win the fight isn't going to be with his lightsaber, but with his ability to rally the freedom fighters to join the Republic and help him defeat the droid army."

# Cham Syndulla
A Twi'lek revolutionary, Cham Syndulla has long opposed Ryloth's leadership. Now he leads the freedom fighters trying to defeat the occupying Separatists.

# GALACTIC DISPATCHES
## HERE COMES THE CAVALRY

All Terrain Recon Transport (AT-RT) pilots such as Stak and Razor play a key role in the invasion of Ryloth, seeking out enemy units on their AT-RTs. AT-RT pilots consider themselves a clone breed apart, doing a dangerous job that demands specialized training.

Get an AT-RT pilot talking and he'll tell you that other clone troopers go to war protected by the armor of AT-TEs, juggernauts, or at least the closed cabins of AT-PTs and AT-XTs, used by the Republic before its military planners decided recon walkers needed an open-cabin design. That open cabin makes AT-RT pilots vulnerable—they sit high in the saddle, exposed to small-arms fire and all too aware that their vehicle's blaster cannon is no match for Separatist vehicles or heavy-infantry droids.

Sure, AT-RT pilots have instruments for scanning terrain, detecting motion, and finding heat sources—but mostly they rely on their eyes and their wits. And they do so while guiding a sometimes-bulky machine across uneven ground, through forests, and even across rivers. To them, maneuvering an AT-RT isn't really driving or piloting, but *riding*—a good pilot knows his AT-RT the way traditional cavalry units know the living creatures they ride.

Other clone troopers sometimes find this attitude a bit much, and mock AT-RT pilots as stilties, scouties, or greenies. But a few minutes behind the stick make them more respectful. For an untrained pilot, just getting the tippy AT-RT to walk smoothly is tough, let alone making it run through uneven terrain while under fire.

# Episode 22:

TIME TO PAY UP, HUTT. I DON'T WORK FOR FREE.

# HOSTAGE CRISIS

"A secret shared is a trust formed."

**Original Airdate:** 3/20/09

**Written by** Eoghan Mahony

**Directed by** Giancarlo Volpe

**Cast**
Corey Burton:
    Cad Bane, Ziro the Hutt,
    Shahan Alama
Matt Lanter:
    Anakin Skywalker
Catherine Taber:
    Padmé Amidala, Betty
    droid
Phil LaMarr:
    Bail Organa, Orn Free Taa,
    Senator Philo
Ian Abercrombie:
    Chancellor Palpatine
Dee Bradley Baker:
    Robonino, Onaconda Farr,
    clone troopers
Matthew Wood:
    Helios-3D, Senate Guard
    #1 & 3, commando droid

## SYNOPSIS

Trapped without his lightsaber, Anakin tries to stop bounty hunter Cad Bane and his band of criminals from seizing control of the Senate building. With Padmé and the other Senators held hostage, Bane demands that Palpatine release Ziro the Hutt from prison. Although Anakin is able to free the captured Senators, he is too late to prevent Cad Bane from getting away with Ziro.

# NEWSREEL

Danger looms! Despite recent victories in the Outer Rim, criminal minds plot at the very heart of the Republic! The bounty hunter Cad Bane has assembled some of the deadliest criminals in the galaxy and plans a daring attack to seize members of the Senate. What can be the aim of this despicable act.... ▮

## MUSTACHE-TWISTING

Did Henry Gilroy enjoy bringing such flamboyant villains as Cad Bane and his bounty-hunting crew to life? Of course he did!

"The contrast between the over-the-top villains and the stoic heroes makes the series fun to write," he says. "Every writer loves to cut loose and allow their villain to be evil to the bone like Bane or Dooku. The great thing about the

## Aurra Sing

A bounty hunter with long limbs and bone white skin, the pitiless Aurra Sing is known as a crack shot with a blaster rifle.

### Cast (Continued)

Tom Kane:
   Senate Guard captain,
   narrator
David Acord:
   Senate Guards, servant
   droid
Anthony Daniels:
   C-3PO
Jaime King:
   Aurra Sing

**Location:** Coruscant

**Vehicles:** Airspeeder, Republic attack gunship

**Weapons:** DC-15A blaster rifle, lightsaber, E-5 blaster rifle, DC-15S blaster, Czerka Adventurer slugthrower rifle, LL-30 blaster pistol

## CHARACTERS

Shahan Alama
Senator Padmé Amidala
Cad Bane
C-3PO
Riyo Chuchi
Onaconda Farr
Helios-3D
Bail Organa
Chancellor Palpatine
Zinn Paulness
Senator Philo
Robonino
Dantum Roohd
Aurra Sing
Anakin Skywalker
Jakker-Sun
Orn Free Taa
Ziro the Hutt

## EPISODE HIGHLIGHT

PUT UP YOUR HANDS.

I GOT BUSINESS WITH THE SENATE.

HOW 'BOUT YOU FELLAS STEP ASIDE?

ON YOUR KNEES AND RAISE YOUR HANDS! SLOWLY!

SON, I WOULDN'T BE SO HASTY IF I WERE YOU.

## MUSTACHE-TWISTING (cont'd)

*Clone Wars* villains is that they have a variety of motivations. Some want money, some power, and others are just killers who [enjoy] the chaos of war. As for the over-the-top killers like Cad Bane and Aurra Sing, you can't help but want the Jedi to take them down and return order to the galaxy. I can't see how the Jedi can possibly be bland if they're going to stop this rogues' gallery of bad guys—it will take all their skill and wits to defeat them."

## TALKING TO HIMSELF

Dave Filoni says the *Clone Wars* creative team tried several versions of Cad Bane's voice in searching for one to suit the pitiless bounty hunter. "In the end, George wanted to go with something that was a little bit off-character," Filoni says, adding that Lucas kept saying, "You can't just make it another Darth Vader—it's too clichéd, it's too predictable."

In the end, Corey Burton came up with "this

weaselly voice for Cad Bane," Filoni says. "If you hear it unaffected, it's actually quite high—a Peter Lorre kind of voice." Filoni, supervising sound editor Matthew Wood, and sound designer David Acord then gave the voice some echo (helped by those tubes on the side of Bane's face) and pitched it "just a tiny bit deeper to add some menace. I think we ended up with something that's not Darth Vader-like, but stands on its own."

Incidentally, when Bane meets Ziro the Hutt, it's Burton providing both voices. "We were fortunate with *Clone Wars* to have very versatile voice actors who can play several roles," Filoni says. "So at the end we have very flamboyant Ziro the Hutt talking to Cad Bane, but it's really just Corey talking to Corey."

## WEAPON PROFILE
### Czerka Adventurer

This long-barreled weapon can fire a variety of ammunition at targets thousands of meters away—but its wielder must have a remarkably steady hand.

## Cad Bane

A deadly Duros bounty hunter, Cad Bane is known for always getting his prey—and for being willing to take on any assignment that pays him enough credits.

## DROID PROFILE
### Betty Droid

BD-3000s are programmed to look and act like young females, and were fashionable on Coruscant during the Clone Wars. They serve Senators and Coruscant's super-rich as attendants.

## WEAPON PROFILE
### Customized LL-30 Blaster Pistol

Used by bounty hunter Cad Bane, the LL-30 blaster pistols have a unique sound when fired and are equipped with a sight along the barrel.

## LESS THAN ZIRO

With his over-the-top mix of malice and cowardice, Ziro the Hutt nearly slithered off with the *Clone Wars* movie. But when it came time for the Hutt's return, Dave Filoni found himself trimming down many of Ziro's lines.

The editing was nothing personal, Filoni insists: "Cad Bane's presence with his crew of bounty hunters was so intense that Ziro's personality kind of softened the whole thing. We wanted to get Ziro out of jail, but we didn't want to do it at the expense of the tension of the story."

If you're disappointed by that, Filoni promises a lot more about Ziro, though not until Season 3: "It's going

to be interesting—the Hutts will be back in *Clone Wars*, that's for sure."

## LETHAL WEAPONS

For Dave Filoni, "Hostage Crisis" represents another instance of *The Clone Wars* getting slowly darker. In "Rising *Malevolence*," we saw Plo Koon stranded with his clone troopers, some of whom didn't survive. In "Rookies," we saw Hevy sacrifice his own life. In "Cloak of Darkness," we saw Captain Argyus betray the Republic—and be betrayed in turn. In "Lair of Grievous," Nahdar Vebb lost his hold on Jedi ideals, and his life. And now we meet new villains whom we instantly realize are a lot more dangerous and sinister than the battle droids.

"I wanted to show a very effective group of bounty hunters," Filoni says. "Cad Bane is a new bounty hunter—he has to be instantly very effective, on the level I always wanted to see Boba Fett work at in the classic trilogy." With Aurra Sing, first glimpsed in *The Phantom Menace*, Filoni "wanted to get across

## Robonino

A pint-sized member of Cad Bane's crew of hunters, Robonino is a skilled slicer who moves quickly to shut down the power in the Senate complex.

## EPISODE HIGHLIGHT

I FEEL IT MY DUTY TO WARN YOU THAT YOU WILL END UP PAYING FOR THIS OUTRAGE.

I CAN LIVE WITH THAT.

## LETHAL WEAPONS (cont'd)

instantly that she is an effective, dangerous weapon—that she is not to be trifled with. We see the IG-series of assassin droids operating more effectively than we've seen them work in the series before. You get to see that short of coming up against a Jedi, these bounty hunters are incredibly dangerous—so dangerous that they take over the entire Senate."

## Ziro the Hutt

Also a crime lord of the Desilijic family, Jabba's flamboyant, but equally dangerous uncle keeps his business centered in Coruscant, rather than the traditional Hutt Space.

# GALACTIC DISPATCHES
## SPRINGING ZIRO

The raid on Ziro the Hutt's Coruscant club foiled a Separatist plot that could have changed the course of the war, and led to a bargain struck by the Republic and the Hutts' Desilijic clan to give Republic warships access to key Hutt routes. Jabba the Hutt was furious to learn his uncle had helped plan the kidnapping of Rotta the Huttlet, and was happy to let Ziro rot in a Republic dungeon.

However, it seems that not everyone was pleased to see Ziro locked away. While it's not clear from this episode who was responsible, someone of considerable means must have hired bounty hunter Cad Bane and his team to rescue the Hutt. And from Chancellor Palpatine's exchange with Bane (where he warns the bounty hunter, "You will end up paying for this outrage"), it seems doubtful that the Separatists are behind this rescue, either. But then again, Darth Sidious's mysterious plans have never been easy to unravel.

As for the Hutt himself, Ziro seems genuinely surprised and a bit taken aback when Bane tells him that it's "time to pay up." Perhaps Ziro initially thought that some loyal member of the Desilijic family has contracted his rescue, but that no longer seem likely — and Ziro knows it.

It seems that Ziro and the rest of us will have to wait until Season 2 to unravel this mystery.

# NEXT STOP: SEASON TWO!

Asked for a tour of his favorite scenes from Season One, Henry Gilroy says that "I loved the Numa scenes with the clones from 'Innocents of Ryloth' because I think we really managed to explore some emotional reality and how war brings out both the worst and the best of human nature. 'Rookies' because we got a sense of how interesting the clones could be. I loved scenes that felt like classic *Star Wars* yet were all new, like the Y-wing attack on the *Malevolence*, Yoda kicking butt on the coral moon, Kit versus Grievous, Luminara and Ahsoka versus Ventress, Artoo's battle with R3-I could go on and on."

Happily, *The Clone Wars* will go on, and Gilroy says that "the stakes will definitely be raised in Season Two. As the second season began animation production, there were more resources to make the stories bigger-that means more ships, more characters, more planets, more everything. We get a glimpse at the past of Obi-Wan that I was thrilled to be a part of, we see some unbelievably diabolical plans of Darth Sidious, and there's the dramatic appearance of some armored bounty hunters who have a large fan following."